Also by Fran Harris

About My Sisters

*Business: The Black Woman's Road Map
to Successful Entrepreneurship*

The Dream Season

IN THE BLACK

The African-American Parent's
Guide to Raising
Financially Responsible Children

FRAN HARRIS

A FIRESIDE BOOK
PUBLISHED BY SIMON & SCHUSTER

This publication contains the opinions and ideas of its author and is
designed to provide useful advice in regard to the subject matter covered.
It is sold with the understanding that the author and publisher are not
engaged in rendering legal, financial, or other professional services. Laws
vary from state to state, and if the reader requires expert assistance or
legal advice, a competent professional should be consulted.

The author and publisher specifically disclaim any responsibility for
liability, loss, or risk, personal or otherwise, that is incurred as a
consequence, directly or indirectly, of the use and application
of any of the contents of this book.

FIRESIDE
Rockefeller Center
1230 Avenue of the Americas
New York, NY 10020

FIRESIDE and colophon are registered trademarks
of Simon & Schuster Inc.

Designed by Pagesetters/IPA

Manufactured in the United States of America

10 9 8 7 6 5 4 3 2 1

Library of Congress Cataloging-in-Publication Data

Harris, Fran, 1965–
In the black : the African-American parent's guide to raising financially
responsible children / Fran Harris.
p.   cm.
"A Fireside book."
1. Afro-American children—Finance, Personal.   2. Children—
Finance, Personal.   I. Title.
HG179.H3184   1998
332.024'03969073—dc21   98-21263
CIP

ISBN 0-684-84338-2

ACKNOWLEDGMENTS

To my family and all of my friends who've supported me in whatever I've done . . . thanks. You know who you are and I love you all.

To my editor and friend, Dawn Daniels, thanks for your professional and personal support.

To all the closet writers out there who haven't yet found the courage to come out . . . go for it! It is a wonderful, exhilarating gift!

AUTHOR'S NOTE
TO THE READER

I've attempted to write this book void of sexist language, so you will see *him, her, he,* and *she* used alternately as much as possible. There will be no *s/he* or *him/her.* It's too cumbersome and it makes for a word-processing and editing nightmare.

Also, I can't keep up with the battle where we go back and forth on whether we want to be called, on any given day, "black" or "African-American," and so forth. So, you will see both of the terms used interchangeably.

CONTENTS

INTRODUCTION

Q. *Mom, I know you said you didn't have any cash, so why can't you just use one of those little plastic cards—maybe that gray one with the blue star on the top?*

A. Boy, have you lost your mind? Do you think money grows on trees?

Think for a second of all the funny things you heard your parents say to you about money: "Girl, do I need to have you committed?" "Boy, you'd better get a job, 'cause you're crazy if you think I'm gonna pay $300 for a jacket for a nine-year-old!" Sound familiar? Money can ignite some of the funniest comments in our households. Unfortunately, sometimes our relationship with money, for all the humor it inspires, contributes to many of our problems as a people. The way we've been encouraged to relate to this necessary resource is what *In the Black* is all about. It's about helping our kids develop healthier relationships with money no matter what our own patterns have been. It's about helping you, the parent, get a grip on your own unique relationship with money so that you can have a positive influence on your child's relationship with it.

Remember what happened when a tooth would fall out of your mouth? The next morning a nice shiny half-dollar would magically appear under your pillow. And we'd sing praises to the tooth fairy, right? Today's kids don't appreciate such niceties. In fact, a half-dollar doesn't go as far as it once did. I used to think that a dollar was big-time money—didn't you? When I'd get a birthday card from an aunt or a grandparent, and that crisp dollar bill would fall out onto the floor, I thought I was in the money. Ah, those were the good old days. Kids nowadays look at you as if you're crazy for even thinking of giving them a dollar for their birthday.

The Winans sing a song that asks us to bring back the days of yea and nay, when things were simple. I wish we could, but let's face it: Our kids are growing up in a time that is anything but simple. Complex and complicated don't begin to tickle the surface of the world our kids are growing up in, so we have to equip them for the realities of their world.

If you're like me, you have a thousand and one things to do from the time you get up in the morning until the second you reach over and turn off the bedside lamp. You may even be saying, "Teach my kids about money? C'mon, Fran, I have enough on my plate already." What I'm asking you to do is about as enticing as going to the dentist. You know you need to do it, but that doesn't make it any easier.

Don't fool yourself. Time isn't the only thing that's stopping you and other black parents from talking to kids about money. Money has never been an easy subject for anyone to discuss. And what's worse is that for us African Americans, the topic has been even more troublesome. Some of our parents have used money as a tool of manipulation, a symbol of affluence or position, a deadly weapon, or a show of love—none of which is an appropriate use for this critical resource. Some sociologists have said that our money woes stem from slavery (the old faithful excuse for all our issues). They claim that our history of deprivation has illuminated the value of money in the black community. While there may certainly be some validity to this theory, there is still no reason for us to continue to pass down unhealthy behaviors. Regardless of the reasons, my hope is that you will address this issue in an aggressive, no-nonsense fashion. And I hope that your children will at least have the chance to walk away with a better grip on their money patterns.

Why I Wrote This Book

The most common question asked of me while I was promoting my book *About My Sister's Business: The Black Woman's Road Map to Successful Entrepreneurship* was "Is there a difference in what black women versus other groups need to know about starting their own businesses?" My answer was a resounding yes. Of course we must deal with different issues. In addition to the basic business start-up concerns, we must also tackle racism, sexism, ageism, and so on. So I wasn't surprised when I was asked the same question when we were planning *In the Black*. There are bookshelves across the country full of books that discuss teaching kids about money, some with sound, helpful advice that can apply to any kid, irrespective of race. But what is missing in those books are the issues that are plaguing black kids on a daily basis—cultural twists, gangs, drugs, racism, and classism, factors that have the capacity to influence our kids' relationship with this important commodity.

When I started writing this book, I began examining my role as money educator in my home. Do I do a good job of instilling good values with my own child? I asked myself. The answer is yes, but I'm still a work in progress and always will be. It takes work and *consistent* effort. I'm as good as I am only because of the mistakes I've made in the past. Isn't experience always the best teacher? So as I continued working on this book, I became even more aware of the areas I wanted to cover to ensure that my daughter would be a smart and savvy money manager, and that I didn't pass on poor habits to her. This book will help other parents discover what I learned: that money education is one of the greatest gifts you can give your child. Let's stop the cycle of mismanagement, misuse, and abuse of money in the African-American community. Let's produce kids who can appreciate a hard day's work and the value of a dollar.

Why You Should Buy This Book

If you want to raise children who have a healthy relationship with money, you should buy this book. If you have identified one or two money demons within yourself that you don't want to pass on to your children, you need this book. If you want your children to develop a sense of confidence where finances and budgets are concerned, this book is for you. In other words, if you have children and are breathing air and reading this page, you would be doing yourself and your children a favor by buying this book.

A word of encouragement: If you're thinking that it's too late because your kids are in their late teen years and set in their ways, let me assure you that it's never too late. Life is a continual learning experience. Just pick up where it's most logical. If your children are facing issues such as running out of recreation money by Wednesday, then start talking to them about budgets and move right along. Opportunity is all around us. Be mindful, though, that you'll need to be as creative with your teenager as you are with your two-year-old. Old habits die hard, but they can and do die. So give it your best shot.

This book does not contain tons of financial jargon and equations. I'm not an economist, nor am I a financial wizard. And you needn't be, either. If you can add two and two, and you're willing to learn something on this journey, then you have nothing to worry about. The good news is that you don't have to work on Wall Street or have a portfolio of stocks, bonds, munis, and CDs to instill solid money values in your children. All you need is a willing heart. And a good dose of patience.

We'll talk budgets, strategy, and planning, but that's about as complicated as the words get. And if you run across a word that you aren't familiar with, do what I do: Pick up a dictionary and carry on. This is not a test. You will not receive grades. Your reward will be kids with good money skills.

Drugs, delinquency, and ignorance are killing our kids more than any other race in America. This book goes beyond money; it's about keeping our kids from falling prey to the lure of gangs and delinquency. It speaks to keeping our kids out of prison and juvenile delinquency homes during the most promising years of their lives. Let's give our kids a fair shot at life. Don't make money the all-consuming goal, as it often is perceived in the African-American community. It's not the reason for being. Let's teach our kids to control the effects of money and not have it control them.

This book boils down to one thing: values. Are you willing to instill in your kids healthy values regarding money? Our children live in a world vastly different from the one you and I grew up in and vastly different from the one many white or brown children grow up in—but that doesn't mean values have changed. Our methods may need a bit of fine-tuning, but good, productive values have basically remained unchanged. But many other things *have* changed. Today, 50 percent of American marriages end in divorce; there's a good chance, then, that you're doing this on your own. You *can* still do it. Furthermore, if *you* don't assume the responsibility of being the primary teacher of sound money values in your household, your kids will learn them from someone else—the neighborhood gang leader, peers, television or other media advertising, and so forth.

I don't know how you feel about this, but I find raising a child in this decade extremely challenging. I really believe we are raising children during the most difficult period of our history. I'm sure our parents felt the same way. The last thing I want is to have my child looking to someone else for *any* major life lessons. Boy! That's scary.

Little eyes see all. It's true. Nothing we do or say as parents gets past our kids, so why not take advantage of the attention we already have? If you steal or fudge, your kids are learning to do the same. If they see you being responsible and attentive with your finances, they'll be more inclined to do the same. And since our kids can either accept or reject the lessons we teach and the examples we set, we should supplement our actions with discussions about the values we're teaching. This way we'll know where our kids' heads are. Teach your kids and teach them well. They will be glad you took the time to care (even the teen-agers who think they know it all), and they will be forever blessed because of it.

Wake Up and Smell the Latte

When my agent was approaching publishers about this book, one of the questions she was asked was "Why do we need a book like this for African Americans?" I found this question laughable. We have our own cultural nuances and, yes, dysfunctions, just like every other group of people. We treat our families in a particular way, we relate to education in our own way, and so forth. Our treatment of money has not escaped. That's why this book is needed. And if those reasons aren't enough, consider the following statistics:

- African Americans have one of the highest debt-to-income ratios in the United States, which means we consistently spend more than we make.
- African Americans have one of the highest credit card debts in the United States, which means we pull out our plastic in a heartbeat.
- A disproportionate number of African-American deaths are related to money, which means that we make these dead presidents too powerful in our communities and homes.

Need I go on?

How to Use This Book

This book is broken down into portions that allow you to get in touch with what you bring to this party—the good, the bad, and the ugly. What are your money strengths and weaknesses? You see, if your grip is not tight, that might explain why your kids are misfits in this area. Plus, we can all sharpen our skills—even those of us who are doing a good job already. The point is to *know*. Remember that '70s commercial "Do you know where your children are"? Well, where money is concerned, my preliminary research shows that we don't have a clue where our kids are. Some of us barely know where *we* are!

This book includes chapters devoted to particular age brackets: preschoolers, preteens, and teenagers. You'll find tools for dealing with money for children who fit into the particular age groups. Also, there are lots of questions, games, and exercises to make this fun. Yes, fun! Learning is fun if you make it that way.

Wouldn't it be nice to know what kind of adults our kids will be. To get a glimpse of this, we have to envision what kind of *child* we want them to become. Once we figure that out, we'll have a better idea of how to help them reach adulthood with the values and money skills we believe are important. This book has exercises with many questions, but there are no right or wrong answers. Your answers will assist you in determining what's important to you and what it is that you want your kids to value.

Here's a chart to help you know what to expect from your kids at different ages. There are no absolutes, so this is just a guide.

Age	Arithmetic	Interest in Money	Possessions	Honesty
2–3	Learning a little about numbers	Enjoys looking at it Fascinated by it May know where to put it (vending machine)	Mine, mine, mine May take things	Doesn't understand yet Beginning to get it
3–4	Counts by ones to ten, twenty	May want to give grocery clerks money	Clearer on what belongs to whom	Better sense of truth
4–5	Can basically add/subtract	Not real strong	Clear about personal property	Learning what's right from wrong
5–8	Multiplication	Starting to develop strongly	Has favorite items	Knows right from wrong
8–11	Division	Strong	May swap with friends	May test boundaries Needs discussions
11–13	Fractions	More activities	Into trading	May flirt with delinquency
13–18	Advanced math Algebra	Higher need for it Definite interest	Wants own money	Ready for serious talks Knows how to manipulate, negotiate, solve problems
	Trigonometry/geometry		Has job	

GETTING STARTED

Household Reality Check: Two Parents, Divorced Parents, and Single Parents

Two parents: If you are fortunate to have some help with your child's money education, be sure you take advantage of it. Don't allow one parent to be the sole educator of anything in your home. Remember in all the movies how the mothers would send their sons to their fathers to have "the talk"? I don't recommend that route at all. Furthermore, think about the roles you and your partner are assuming and what messages your kids are getting. Are you the one who cooks, cleans, or disciplines all the time? Think about it. Money is a subject that should be discussed by and with both parents.

Divorced parents: It's important that you and your ex understand each other's money philosophies. Money will creep into your conversations with your kids, and when it does, you must be ready. Never criticize how your ex handles money in front of your children. If you have an issue with a decision that your ex has made, go to him or her—not the kids. It's important to discuss the goals you have for your children and that you each cooperate to carry out the plan. If one parent has a loosey-goosey approach to money and the other parent has a more disciplined agenda in mind, you resolve this gap in philosophies by talking and agreeing on methods. And most important, remember, this is about what's best for the kids, not you.

Single parents: If you are doing this alone, you may not have to worry about another influential person botching up your hard work. Then the thing to watch out for is fatigue. Single parents have the complete load on their shoulders, and sometimes it's not that you don't care about an important task, it's that you are flat-out tired. Fortunately, with money, if you lay the right foundation, it's self-sustaining. This does not mean that once you teach your kids about money they no longer need you. Hardly. But if you communicate your values clearly, concisely, and consistently, your kids will help you help them. They'll ask good questions and sometimes solve problems without intervention. So don't worry if you're singing solo; follow the guidelines in this book, and you won't miss a beat.

Prosperity and Wealth

Prosperity doesn't necessarily mean wealth, although it could include it. "Prosperity is a state of striving and thriving, success, and good fortune." Notice that I said nothing about money in that definition. I'm living a prosperous life these days; I could use a little more money, though I have all the money I need. There's a tricky statement: I have all the money I need. What does that mean? For me it means that my obligations are met. That I'm not two paychecks from being homeless. For you, it might mean that you have no creditors. That you have arranged your life so that you can take off and go to Europe for two months if the right offer comes along. For me, it means that I can drive to Fredricksburg, Texas, where the sweetest, most delicious peaches grow, and eat them until I'm nauseous. That, to me, is prosperity.

To others, prosperity may be measured by the number of digits on their paychecks. Or the number of cars parked in the driveway. Or the clothes in the closet. Or the number of rings on the fingers, and so forth. *Prosperity is a state of thriving*. I like this. Are you thriving? Would you say that you lead a prosperous life? An abundant existence? Do you want your kids to emulate the life you lead? I want my daughter's life to be even better. She has a good example, but I don't want her to trip up on the same obstacles as her mother. I want her to do it the easy way.

Webster says wealth is having riches and affluence, and affluence is having an abundance of riches, thoughts, and power. Do we want this for our kids? Why not? Wealth is not evil, and it's not reserved for certain people. But if my daughter asked me whether I'd choose to be wealthy or prosperous, I'd take prosperity over wealth any day. Why? Because prosperity seems to be a lifestyle. It's a direct result of W-O-R-K! You can be born into wealth and not know how to accumulate more of it or what to do with what you have. But if we instill in our kids the importance of developing strong work habits, they can achieve phenomenal wealth, position, and power—if they so desire.

In the Black was designed to help you lead your children to a life of financial responsibility, independence, and abundance.

The School of Hard Knocks

The first thing you have to ask yourself is where *your* money education came from. Second, you must admit that your ideas about money came from the authority figures in your home—parents, grandparents, aunts, uncles, and so forth. Your money sense probably includes some good habits but also some bad habits that you don't want to pass along to your children. Whether you know it or not, you were getting an education when your parents talked about grocery money or school clothes. Remember what those conversations were like? Think back to one of the earliest conversations your parents had about money. I'll give you an example.

A nine-year-old is sitting at the table doing homework when her dad comes home from work. Mom says, "I need money for school clothes." Dad looks at her and never changes his expression. He reaches into his grimy overalls and pulls out a wad of bills. He unfolds them and counts them out into Mom's hand. She looks at the bills and smiles. "Have you looked at her lately? She's not a baby anymore. This ain't gon' get it."

Dad walks to the kitchen and peeps into the pots. "That's all I got," he says.

"That's [expletive meaning she doesn't quite buy it]. This'll get me started, but I'm going to need some more soon."

"I said that's all I have," Dad says, his voice getting louder.

Here are a few things I took from that exchange. Daddy brought home the money, and whatever he decided was enough was what he gave Mom for whatever the request was. People sometimes lie about money. When they say they have one thing, they could have another. Those were the messages I got.

Now it's your turn. Write a story from your past. Don't interpret it, just recount.

_____

_____

_____

_____

_____

_____

_____

Write the messages that you got from this.

_____

_____

_____

Can you see how a similar exchange might influence how your kids respond in comparable situations?

If Not You, Who?

African-American kids today have much more contact with money and money-related issues than you or I probably did, and money seems to have a more important role in their social environments. Learning money skills is therefore critical for them. And, believe me, if you don't teach your children money skills, they'll learn them somewhere else.

You must go beyond yelling at your child when she takes money from your purse. Keep in mind some possible consequences. I read recently that almost all kids "experiment" with shoplifting, so you can't assume that just because you've never received a call about picking your kids up from a store or a police station that they haven't engaged in this delinquent behavior. Talk to your children. Ask them questions. You'll be surprised at what goes on in those minds. And please avoid judging them.

If you never take the time to sit down and initiate a conversation about money, your kids may grow up to be financial misfits—incapable of handling money, building nest eggs, and securing a future. If you don't think it's important to develop a plan that will enable your child to understand money and all its uses, just think about the many inmates in prisons across the country who are serving time for money-related crimes.

WHAT ABOUT THE CHURCH?

Unfortunately, many churches (please note that I did not say *all* churches) have failed miserably at improving our relationship with money. In many instances they have perpetuated the myth about money's correlation with wrongdoing or sin. As a result, many black folks believe that money is the root of all evil—or the love of money is the root of all evil, depending on who is preaching that Sunday. Some ministers openly recognize people who give large sums of money to the church or scrutinize those who do not do so. What message does that send to children?

Many religions teach that God requires us to give a portion of all we earn to the church. This is a good lesson about charity and moral responsibility, but what happens when clergy try to instill guilt in congregations?

WHAT ABOUT THE SCHOOL SYSTEM?

In general, schools do a horrendous job of teaching children about how money flows through our society. Is there a course entitled Household Economics 101 in your school district? Not in mine. Most schools do a good job of teaching arithmetic but nothing about money management, budgets, and balancing check-books. Schools need to start teaching money skills because many kids leave high school with little or no knowledge of this important subject.

TRUE STORY

A fifteen-year-old girl arrives home from school wearing a new pair of jeans, sneakers, and jacket. The father asks where it all came from. The daughter replies, "I got paid." She was selling drugs, bringing in over $3,000 a week. Two weeks later she was dead. She was getting paid, all right, but don't you think the cost was too high?

What Are Your Goals for Your Kids?

When it comes to *your* goals for your kids, we're not necessarily talking about college or medical school just yet. We're talking about psychological goals. Do you want them to covet money or have a "take it or leave it" attitude, or something in between? Do you want them to be brand-name conscious? Do you want them to purchase Tommy Hilfiger or the sensible pair of good-looking jeans for half the price?

Once you get past those goals, ask yourself the following: Do you want them to go to college? Would you like them to get a taste of entrepreneurship as children? Use the space below to write your goals for them. Remember, goals must be specific and measurable.

_____

_____

_____

_____

_____

_____

_____

_____

At age twelve, one year after my oldest brother, Alonzo, bought me a subscription to _Black Enterprise,_ I sat and wrote a list of goals that I wanted to achieve before my life was over. I wasn't ill or anything, just ambitious. At the top of my list was to own my own business. Next was to be an anchor on television. Next, I wanted to be a writer. And, finally, I wanted to retire by age thirty. Why thirty? I have no idea. But I figured I'd go to college at seventeen, get an undergraduate degree, and then do whatever it was my sister was doing (maybe get a master's). I'd play basketball for as long as I could, and I'd travel.

My brother said my goals could and probably would change. I remember his asking me about money, about financial goals. I looked at him and said, "Money? I'm not worried about money. One day soon I'll have plenty of that."

What Is Money?

Maybe this sounds like an obvious question, but you need to see your answers in front of you. So jot down everything you think money is or means in your own words. Don't edit. Just write whatever comes to your mind. You don't have to make complete sentences or even follow a stream of thought. Just write!

_____

_____

_____

Look at the words you used to describe money. Do you have any feelings about any of the words you used? If you have a spouse, it would be interesting to compare your answers. Think about how your answers manifest themselves in behaviors. For instance, if you perceive money as power, you might exhibit the behavior of insisting on maintaining control of your joint checkbook, never allowing your spouse to review it.

A HISTORICAL LOOK AT US AND MONEY

There is a possibility that we are not keenly aware of our relationship with money. So I included this section for two reasons: as a wake-up call or a reminder (you decide which is appropriate for you). But just remember, your children are the issue here. The clearer you are about your own habits and patterns, the more effective you will be in developing healthy money habits in your children. Now, let me add one tiny disclaimer. It's possible that you grew up in a household with parents who never fought about money, who both worked, who gave you and your siblings allowances, and who talked openly and honestly about finances and money. If this is the case, congratulations, you are a minority. Because the reality is that, like sex and death, money has fallen prey to the Hush Syndrome in many African-American homes—it's simply not discussed in a manner that would create a healthy relationship with it. Hence, we don't always feel comfortable discussing it with our spouses, friends, or kids. We're not even always comfortable having it in our pockets. But no matter what kind of home environment you had, you still have a chance to raise youngsters who are smart money managers.

This section gets to the heart of some of our money woes, the traps that keep us in an impoverished mindset. The traps that, if we are not careful, our kids fall into as they head into adulthood. Keep in mind that this list is only a sample; it is not exhaustive, by any means. Finally, keep an open mind, and, most of all, be honest with yourself. Your kids deserve your best effort.

TRAP NUMBER 1: BECOMING A VICTIM OF PLASTIC MANIA

Yes, credit cards help us build credit, an important facet of today's world. They afford us more financial flexibility. The key word is *flexibility*, which connotes that there are *choices*. What has happened to us is that we think that because we *have* plastic, that we must *use* it. That's the psychology of credit cards. That's why we have one of the highest credit delinquency rates in the country. We've fallen hook, line, and sinker for the hype. Please don't misunderstand me. Establishing credit is essential. And good credit is a luxury not to be taken for granted. But credit cards are to *be* handled delicately. Their uses should be limited. Credit cards are most helpful in *making reservations* for things, such as hotels, trips, and rental cars. You really should pay cash for these expenses, or pay the credit card bill in total once you receive it. Credit cards are *not* a substitute for money.

Behavior: Your kids have listened to you gripe all week long about not having a penny to your name. So what do you do? You go shopping, and when you return with bags full of clothes, your kids are confused. They ask how you can buy clothes without money. You tell them you used your credit cards.

Message to kids: That it's possible to spend money that you *don't* have.

New Behavior: If you truly don't have money in your checking account, don't send an unhealthy money message by splurging with your plastic. Your kids are likely to follow in your footsteps. Plastic is the best way to mess up your credit and put you into financial strain.

TRAP NUMBER 2: LIVING BEYOND YOUR MEANS

This is a big one. We oughta write a story about the most creative stories we tell creditors. I bet it would be a best-seller. We get in the pool and don't realize we're drowning until the paramedics arrive. We must develop skills to prevent us from getting in over our heads, which would help our kids avoid doing the same.

Behavior: Your sorority sisters come into town, and it's going to be girls' night out. Everybody's having breakfast at Shug's, then off to the spa for a full day of beauty, lunch, a matinee, followed by dinner at Chez Some-body's. The only thing is that you know you can't afford it. But guess what? You're goin' anyway, right? Right. Big mistake—spending what you ain't got just to keep up with everybody else.

Message to kids: Everybody else is doing it, so I gotta be with the gang—no matter how much debt (or the consequences) I incur, no matter what it takes.

New behavior: Plan ahead. Let your kids know that in order to have anything worthwhile, you have to work for it. Start talking about your big day or event as soon as you are committed to having or doing it. Let your kids see you put a plan in motion where you're setting money aside and making personal sacrifices to achieve this goal.

Trap Number 3: Keeping Up with the Jacksons

This is similar to number 2, but is a constant need to have what everybody else has.

Behavior: If you hear or see that a relative or neighbor is getting a new recreational vehicle, you rush out to du-plicate this feat. Sometimes bigger and better.

Message to kids: What we have is never enough or good enough. We don't set our own standards; they're dic-tated by someone else. Never be outdone.

New behavior: When someone else gets a new toy, let your kids see you express genuine joy for someone else. Call up your cousin and congratulate her on her new acquisition . . . and mean it. Reiterate to your kids that when you work hard, you should reward yourself. Also, let them know that the reward does not have to be monetary or material.

Trap Number 4: Ignoring Money Problems

Okay, so you get behind on your phone bill. Just because you're pretending to forget doesn't mean the phone company will.

Behavior: You let the bills pile up on the table unopened. Nobody says anything. You don't. Your spouse doesn't.

Message to kids: They see irresponsibility. They know that the phone isn't free (I hope you've at least told them this). They may think that if you ignore a problem, it will go away without any assistance from the person accountable for it.

New behavior: Let your kids know that emergencies arise, and it's not always possible to meet your responsibilities as you would like but that the responsible way to act is to be accountable. Let your kids hear you setting up a payment plan with the phone company so they understand that many things in life are negotiable and that you don't have to contribute to a seemingly desperate situation by ignoring your responsibility. Let them know that if you don't call the phone company, they *will* call you or, worse, terminate your service.

Trap Number 5: Getting Overwhelmed

You know you won't have the entire amount of your electric bill because you've missed two weeks of work due to illness.

Behavior: Don't open the mail. Don't answer calls from the electric company. You ask your kids to say you're not home. Lie in bed all day. Depression kicks in.

Message to kids: Problems aren't too bad if you act as if they don't exist.

New behavior: Set up an emergency fund for such occasions.

TRAP NUMBER 6: MISMANAGEMENT

Behavior: I have a friend who received a six-figure settlement for an accident and, believe me, her husband couldn't wait for that check to get there. And when it arrived, her eyes were the size of a pair of golf balls! They had that money spent already. How long do you think it took her and her husband to spend it? Less than six months. Now, you tell me that wasn't foolish. They could have done a million constructive things with that money—decreasing their debt being one of them—but instead she and her spouse blew it.

Message to kids: Don't let money sit too long. Get rid of it as quickly as possible.

New behavior: Have a formal meeting to plan how the money will be used. Discuss savings, investing, and spending percentages.

TRAP NUMBER 7: NOT PAYING FOLKS WHEN YOU CAN

Behavior: You get into debt, so you borrow from family and friends. You get hurt on your job and get a huge settlement. You buy a new car, some new clothes for your kids, go to the casino, and so forth.

Message to kids: Don't honor your obligations. Have fun with your money and don't fulfill responsibilities to the people who helped you when you couldn't help yourself.

New behavior: Make a list of the people you owe, then arrange to pay them back in a sensible manner. But do pay them back.

Trap Number 8: Spreading the Wealth

Behavior: Remember my friend in Trap Number 6? Well, she was the samaritan who gave thousands of dollars to family and friends. Yep. She wanted to share her abundance. I have nothing against charity or sharing, but not before you've taken care of yourself and your own. And even after you've taken care of you, be sensible. A $10,000 gift is a bit extravagant for somebody who only has $100,000.

Message to kids: We have to help others to our own detriment. In other words, everybody else is eating except us.

New behavior: Limit gifts. Generosity is rewarded, but carelessness with your money will get you nowhere.

Trap Number 9: Not Saving for a Rainy Day

When emergencies arise, who are ya gonna call? Ghostbusters can't help you here. That's why we need to get better at building our emergency funds. Experts say that you should have at least six months' cash reserved for emergencies. At least. Do you? Some of us don't have six days!

Behavior: Your spouse becomes ill and can't work for two months. His insurance won't give disability because of his specific condition. Your household is short $1,500 a month. You're stressed, your spouse is stressed, and, yes, your kids are stressed!

Message to kids: Don't plan for the unexpected. Live life day to day. Things work out.

New behavior: Establish a rainy day account.

A Test to Discover Your Money IQ

Thought this was a book for your kids? It is, but how can you help your kids if you can't help yourself? This test is critical because it will help you identify your strengths and weaknesses with money. This will, in turn, help you help your children have a healthier experience with it. You are to answer in the way in which you are "most likely" to respond. Let's continue.

1. Your six-year-old daughter loses her thirty-five cents for milk. You:

   a. give her another thirty-five cents.
   b. let her do chores to make up the money.
   c. tell her to be more careful next time.

2. Your fifteen-year-old star athlete has been saving her allowance for months. When she has saved up to $200, she wants to buy Michael Jordan's latest sneakers. You:

   a. let her buy them.
   b. laugh and say, "You're really tripping if you think I'm letting you pay $200 for some sneakers."
   c. tell her she can't touch her savings.

3. You tell your thirteen-year-old son to clean his room. He says, "I'll do it if you pay me." You:

    a. whip out your wallet and sling him a $5 bill.
    b. give him "that" look and walk away.
    c. tell him that cleaning his room is not a job, it is his responsibility as a member of the family.

4. Your nine-year-old wants a glitzy (cheap but popular) backpack collection that you believe will fall apart before she gets it out of the car and up the school steps. You:

    a. let her buy it herself.
    b. buy it for her since you're buying all the school supplies anyway.
    c. tell her to forget it, you're getting her the one you want her to have.

5. Your seventeen-year-old announces he's going out for a while and casually asks you for $10. You:

    a. roll your eyes and ask him if he's lost his mind.
    b. give it to him and keep watching TV.
    c. tell him it comes out of his allowance as previously agreed.

6. It's your preschooler's birthday, and she has asked for a Sega Genesis something or other. You explain there's no way that she's getting that gift; it's not in the budget. But it mysteriously arrives in the mail from Nana in North Carolina. You:

    a. grit your teeth and shut your mouth (after all, it is your mother).
    b. tell Mom your daughter can't accept it.
    c. thank your mother but tell her that in the future she should talk to you before sending pricey gifts to the kids.

7. Your son receives $50 in the mail as a birthday gift. You:

   a. let him splurge on whatever he wants.

   b. remind him that all money that comes in the house must be distributed to the appropriate banks as previously agreed.

   c. take it away from him; you need it.

8. Your five-year-old asks what would happen to him if you died. You:

   a. tell him to stop asking silly questions, that nothing's going to happen to you.

   b. tell him he'd probably go and live with Aunt Debra (even though you don't have a will and haven't talked to your sister about this).

   c. ask him how he would feel about living with Aunt Debra if something happened to you (your will states that she will have custody).

9. Both your daughter and son come home from school and say that they've been asked to join the school's most notorious gang. The leader shoved a $100 bill at both of them. You:

   a. ask them why they're standing there without the loot.

   b. take them out of that school and send them to another.

   c. ask them how they felt about their experience and if they had any inclination to say yes or why they said no.

10. Your daughter finds a $10 bill on the bus on the way home. You:

   a. take it away and tell her she did the right thing by keeping it.

b. let her keep it.

c. ask her if she made any effort to find the owner; if not, you ask her how she plans to get it back to the rightful owner.

11. Your son is off to college at the end of the summer. He says he spent almost all his money from his summer job. You:

    a. promise him a weekly allowance.
    b. tell him that's too bad, that them that's got shall get.
    c. sit him down to discuss what he has in savings and his getting a job during school, and that you will consider supplementing him with a small allowance.

12. Your four-year-old is usually very well behaved at the grocery store with you, but today she threw a tantrum and cried incessantly. You:

    a. interrupt your shopping to take her outside to wear that little butt out.
    b. explain to her that you need for her to behave, or you may have to leave her home next time.
    c. allow her to choose one item.

13. Your son comes to you on Wednesday and tells you that he has run out of lunch money. You:

    a. spot him the money.
    b. tell him you'll advance him the money.
    c. tell him he needs to see what he can scrounge up in the kitchen to take in a brown bag.

14. R. Kelly is making a rare appearance in your city. Your daughter is on restriction for bringing home poor grades, plus she doesn't have enough money for the ticket in her spending account. You:

   a. make an exception and advance her the money;
     after all, it is the "R."
   b. keep a straight face and tell her she made the bed
     she's lying in.
   c. tell her she can go if she can find the money, but
     you're not giving it to her.

15. The Chicago Bulls are playing the Houston Rockets, and your fourteen- and fifteen-year-olds have received tickets from a buddy. They've also been invited to a postgame party where there may be drugs, liquor, and celebrities, including a few of the players. You:

   a. tell them to live large while they can.
   b. go to the game with them and escort them to the
     party (cause you wanna meet Mike, Dennis, Pip,
     Sir Charles, and The Dream).
   c. tell them that curfew is extended to compensate
     for the late game but you expect them to be
     home no later than that extension.

16. A local businessperson has agreed to mentor your child and begins to give lavish gifts on a monthly basis. You:

   a. say nothing because you like having something
     to brag about on bowling nights.
   b. tell your kids not to forget to write a thank-you
     note.
   c. contact the person to express your sincere
     thanks but explain that you're trying to instill
     certain values and you think a monthly gift is an
     extravagance. You'd be happy to send a list of
     important dates in case the person wants to do
     something for those special occasions.

SCALE AND SCORING

If you selected more than 10 a's or b's, individually or combined, we need to talk. Better yet, you're in for a long, rocky road if you keep this pace.

If you had between 5 and 9 a's or b's, you could use more backbone and discipline in your household. Your kids are not sure where you stand, and, believe me, they want to know.

If you had between 1 and 4 a's or b's, you're definitely heading in the right direction. We all let up sometimes, but remember: Our kids will benefit more from structure and consistency. Keep up the good work!

TAKE CONTROL OF YOUR MONEY NOW!
BE LIKE DON!

How many of us would do what Don Calhoun did in 1983? Don Calhoun was just a regular working fella when he went to a Chicago Bulls game. At halftime he sank a half-court shot and won a million dollars. I'm scared to ask, but what would you have done had you won a million bucks?

The next day Don was interviewed by Bryant Gumbel on the *Today Show*. When asked what he was going to do with the money, he said he wanted to send his daughter to college. He immediately called on the services of someone who could help him make his money "grow" or work for him. What Don did is exactly what you and I need to get better at. There are three things we can do with our money: save it, invest it, or spend it.

I'm reminded of the parable of the father who gave his three servants two coins each. The first servant went out and risked his money and doubled it. The next servant invested it and doubled it as well. The third servant, with all good intentions, took his money and saved it. Now which of these individuals do you think won the favor of his father? Right: the two who made their money *make* money.

But wait a minute, you say. I thought saving was a good thing. It is. But investing is a better thing. Let's say I give you $50. In ten years that $50 will be $50 if you stick it under your pillow. But if you take it and put it in an interest-bearing account, it'll be at least $75 in ten years. If you buy a U.S. Savings Bond, it'll be worth more than its face value in ten years. You get my point. Investing is a form of saving. In fact, it's a tool to help you build on the money you have. We'll talk more about this later, but for now, I want you to get in the mindset of making your money and your kids' money work. If you adopt this mindset, so will your kids.

What Kind of Money Manager Are You Today?

Learning what kind of manager *you* are might give you some idea of your child's predisposition. Let's take a look at how you relate to your own money by reviewing the following African-American Parent Profiles:

Wall Streeter: You got the checkbook balanced to the letter, and nothing fires you up like watching your investments grow. You take pride in being better at banking than anyone else. To you, money means security.

The Great Pretender: You have all the "thangs" to make you appear to be all that—the cars, the jewelry, the house and pool. But you're scrounging to pay your bills, and you know it. You and your spouse probably don't see eye to eye on how you wheel and deal the money. For you, money means clout, position, advantage.

The Tightwad: You know who you are. Your nickname is Squeakers. You find it difficult to spend money. You claim to be a saver, but deep down you're really afraid you'll end up penniless.

The Consummate Entertainer: Happy hour is your time to shine. You buy rounds for the gang and wonder where all your loot is when the fifteenth of the month rolls around. Every holiday you have a party at your place; no potluck for you—you cover the whole thing.

The Money Martyr: You feel bad or anxious if you have too much money, so you spend and give freely instead of making smart money decisions. You may believe that God doesn't want you to have too much.

The Money Manic: You worry about not having enough. You never have enough even when you do. You're constantly balancing your checkbook and doing your taxes in January.

The Money Avoider: You're the person who's driving downtown at 11:59 P.M. on April 15 to turn in your taxes. You don't wanna fight about it. You don't wanna talk about it. Just take it. Here, take all my money.

So what happens when two of these profiles meet each other? Is it "look out!" time? No, not really. Being different is good; you can help each other grow. Balance is the key, not dominance. The point is not to change each other or to wear each other down; don't manipulate your partner into doing things your way. The trick is to find a happy medium. We never feel totally good about losing a complete part of ourselves, but compromising is healthy, so give it a try. If you don't invest in some serious communication efforts, you could be in trouble. Conflict may be certain and inevitable, but that doesn't mean it's unhealthy. The important thing is to identify your profile right now and then be open to developing the skills that will promote a healthy balance in your children.

Sound Familiar?

PARTNER 1 (Money Manic): See, this is why we don't have money at the end of the month. You're always buying stuff we don't need.

PARTNER 2 (The Entertainer): And you are so anal we never have fun money.

Don't be fooled into thinking that the Entertainer is the bad one in this scenario. The Money Manic may be holding on so tight to the money that the relationship is smothering to death. If this kind of dialogue is common in your household, you and your mate need to sit down and develop goals. Most couples who report having a healthy relationship about money are those who have a bills account set up for payment, and they each get an allowance. Yeah! Allowances work for adults, too. Try it!

Honesty Is the Only Policy

Your kids already know your attitudes about money. No matter how clever you think you are, you can't hide your attitudes; they show up with little or no effort. Your kids may not understand where your issues stem from, but they've definitely witnessed your behavior enough to know if Dad's a penny pincher or a big spender. Recently I wanted to get my dad to increase his insurance coverage. When my mom died in 1981, her policy barely covered the cost of burial. So when my father showed me his insurance policy, I knew I had to do something about it because we didn't want our family to be up a creek following his death. I grew up with this man and always knew that he didn't part with his money well. I briefly forgot that my father grew up poor (or, as he says, "po"), which plays a big part in how he deals with money. My dad is one of the hardest working people I know, and he has made tons of money as his own boss. But he's never known how to make his money work for him or really how to save for the long term.

I planned a trip home and called the insurance agent to come over to my dad's after Sunday dinner. I knew I had my work cut out for me, and I had already fine-tuned my sales pitch based on my knowledge of his profile. And I was right. Dad wasn't interested in hearing it, but eventually I convinced him that for an additional $20 a month he could save us a lot of stress when he leaves this world. He didn't go for an increase that would have resulted in a $50 monthly increase, but he did meet me somewhere in the middle. He felt empowered and I felt relieved, so we both came out winners.

Does Honesty Spill Over into Bad News?

Q. *I lost my job, and I don't know how to handle it with my kids. I feel sure that I can line something up real soon but in the meantime money will be beyond tight. How much should I share with them?*

A. Enough to include them but not so much that they can't function in their daily lives. Losing a job is a serious obstacle, and they will know that something is up with you, so rather than taking it out on them or exploding for some other reason, it's best to be up front. Your kids need to know that sometimes life serves up a bowl of cherry pits! And when it does, support comes in handy. That's right: Ask your kids to support you, and they will feel more empowered even in this seemingly disempowering situation.

HOW OPEN SHOULD I BE WITH MY KIDS ABOUT SALARIES?

Do your kids need to know how much money you make? Not necessarily. A five-year-old can't appreciate a $50,000 salary, and I'm not sure what the point of telling your sixteen-year-old would be. Divulging salaries is tricky because you don't want your youngster to use the information the wrong way—such as blabbing to the wrong crowd that his mom brings home a $6,000 check on the first of each month. You could be inviting crime into your home. Plus, you want to encourage your children to be proud of the fruits of their labor but never to be show-offs.

Here is a valuable exercise for kids of all ages. Ask your kids how much they think it costs to run a household. Get on your computer or write out by hand a list of all the expenses connected with running a house. This is your list. Get your kids around the table one night after dinner, give them a blank sheet of paper, and ask them to list the household expenses—as many as they can come up with. (Don't tell them that you have the master list.) Your goal is to see how in tune they are with reality. Once they've made their lists, give them each a copy of the real deal. It'll be fun. It's normal for kids to have only a third of what's on your list. That's part of the exercise. After you give them the master list, ask them to put a monthly amount next to the expenses you've listed. Once again they will probably have no clue. Once they have finished, bring 'em back into reality one more time. Congratulations! You have just completed a very important lesson that should make your children more aware and sensitive to money issues. If one of your kids says, "Yeah, so what?," then you need to worry and seek help. Do not pass Go, and definitely leave the $200 in the bank.

Protecting Kids from the World's Harsh Realities

It's noble to want to protect your kids from harsh realities, but it doesn't help them develop into healthy adults. Let's say your phone service gets terminated because you forgot to pay the bill. Your son tries to call you to ask you to pick him up from band practice, but he can't get you. He keeps getting the "I'm sorry, the number you have reached . . ." recording. You pull up in the car, and what do you tell him? That the phone company must have made a mistake because you would never miss a payment? That there's been a power outage in the area and the service will be restored tomorrow? Wrong on both counts. You tell the truth. Yes, the bitter truth. Your kids need to understand what happens when you fail to meet your obligations. Your kids need to know that you make mistakes, too. And, most important, they need to know that you hold yourself accountable for your goof-ups. These are three great lessons for any child. Don't deprive your child of these lessons because you're too proud or embarrassed to admit you're human.

> Q. *I was passed over for a raise, and I believe with all my heart it's because I'm black. How do I share my pain with my kids without encouraging them to blame racism for everything?*
>
> A. First of all, even if your kids can't talk very well yet, they pick up on your moods, your emotions. They know! Second, if you have school-aged kids, the key is to be honest about how you *feel*. Focus on using sentences that show

how you feel. "I feel so unappreciated. I've been with the company for ten years. I've done good work, and I'd like to be recognized for it." Not: "I tell you what—a black man in this world can't get a break." Even if you feel that way, you don't want your kids to approach the world with this attitude. By expressing your *feelings*, your kids will see a behavior that's honest and vulnerable, not blaming.

DO AS I SAY AND NOT AS I DO

Over the holidays a beautiful and well-mannered two-year-old, Chastity, is minding her own business when a visitor starts playing with her. Goo goo, gah gah. She is not interested in these juvenile games; after all, she's playing with her new Tickle Me Elmo. The stranger continues until finally the two-year-old turns to him and says, "Don't *@%# with me!"

Don't tell me our kids don't pick up on everything we say and do. They watch our body language, they listen to our intonation. So be careful. This child's parent was mortified, but I told her that she shouldn't be embarrassed but should use this incident as motivation to set a better example for her child.

How We Influence Our Children

Attitude: How we feel about something. Which values do you want to instill in your kids? Example: optimism.

Facts: There are certain things that just are. Yes, just are. There's nothing we can do about how laws work or how credit works, so these are the kinds of facts that we want our kids to learn. Example: Banks sometimes charge for check-writing privileges.

Skills: Things we learn to do. Examples include budgeting and making change.

Habits: These are what we want to become permanent parts of our kids' behavioral patterns. Saving, investing, and goal-setting are examples.

Kids learn at different paces. Don't get frustrated if they don't get it at first. Keep churning away, and they'll get it. Also remember that kids, especially younger ones, learn by experimenting, touching, *not* from listening to you lecture.

How to Make Learning a Positive Experience

Here are a few tips for making this journey work for you and your kids.

1. Treat your kids with dignity. We black parents sometimes get a bad rap. Folks think we don't know how to talk to our kids; they think we yell instead. Some of us do. If you are a yeller, work on developing better communication skills. You want your kids to hear the message. When yelling is the only mode of communication, sometimes kids miss the message. Sometimes we grownups miss it, too!

2. Don't ridicule and name-call. There's no faster way to break a child's spirit than with negative reinforcement. Black kids will hear enough negative messages about themselves in their lifetime. Don't be a part of the negativity. Saying such things as "You're so stupid" or "Why do I always have to go over things twice with you?" are killers. Don't say these things to your kids—even if someone has said them to you. Break the cycle.

3. Don't compare kids—to yourself or to anyone else. Saying "Your brother was doing this when he was just five years old" can create unnecessary and misdirected anger between ordinarily loving siblings. And don't say, "You're slow just like your mother. She never could count to ten herself." These comments not only damage esteem; they also create negative images of another person.

4. Praise and recognize. It's important to praise twice as often as you provide constructive feedback. Make sure you use every opportunity to say, "Good job" or "Way to go!" And a big one is, "You're so good at ———."

5. Give 'em love and support. Hug and kiss your kids. Give them high fives. Find creative ways to support and honor their progress. Make certificates or give them ribbons. I find a reason to praise my daughter on her money skills development almost every week.

Kudos Alert

When your kids start prefacing "begging sessions" with "Mom, I was wondering if a movie is in our budget this week," give yourself a pat on the back because you're heading in the right direction. I don't know about you, but this is music to my ears!

THE PRECIOUS
PRESCHOOLERS

Ages One to Five

"Mom, who is that man on your money?"

If your child is learning to speak or is identifying fruit or the letters of the alphabet, there's a money lesson you can teach. And before you start whining about how little time you already have, talking to kids about money doesn't necessarily mean you have to have a full-scale seminar every night, complete with overheads and notes; in fact, quality is definitely more important than quantity here.

Think about all the skills your kids have already learned as toddlers—brushing their teeth, combing their hair, and taking a bath. A two-year-old may not completely understand the importance of good hygiene, but you wouldn't wait until she is six to teach her to brush her teeth, would you (although I'm told that flossing is a skill some parents delay teaching)? I hope not. You teach the skill first; learning the reasons behind the skill is an ongoing process. The same principle applies to money lessons: Teach the habit and explain as you go.

You should devote at least an hour a week to Money 101. That's nothing compared to the dividends you'll receive on your investment. It doesn't have to be one concentrated hour—although that would be ideal—but, say, fifteen minutes after dinner or twenty minutes after school or before bedtime a few nights a week. Bedtime is an excellent opportunity to teach money skills because kids love bedtime stories. Just decide on a lesson and then make up a story around it. Your kids will not only benefit from getting your attention but will also learn a valuable lesson.

Here's a story your young ones will enjoy.

One day, Papa Bear was taking little Baby Bear to the grocery store to buy dinner for Mama Bear's birthday. Papa Bear asked Baby Bear what he thought Mama Bear might enjoy for her birthday dinner. Baby Bear thought and thought. Then his eyes got as big as two saucers, and he said, "Hot dogs! Mommy loves hot dogs!"

Papa Bear asked Baby Bear to help him find all the things they needed to buy for the dinner. He made a deal: "I'll drive the cart, and you show me what Mommy likes to eat with her hot dogs."

This story can also include discussion of brands (for older children) and prices and brand comparison. It can be upgraded to meet just about any child's development needs. Have fun!

Common Money Misconceptions Among Blacks

I took an informal survey (which means I asked every friend who would talk to me about money) concerning the most common money ghosts among our people, and here's what I found. Those who responded asked not to be identified, so the names have been omitted to protect the embarrassed.

Too much money is risky/bad. Some of the people I talked to said that they thought this ghost was at work because so many black folks had their checks spent before they ever reached the bank to cash them.

People with money are bad, not to be trusted. When powerful people go sour, we think somehow it was money that made them turn to a life of crime. When we see one black person corrupted by money, we may immediately think the acquisition of the money changed their behavior. That money alone turned them from good human beings to bad ones. In other words, the belief is that money is truly the root of evil.

I'm supposed to be poor. C'mon! We were never "supposed" to be poor. Sometimes we forget that abundance is rightfully ours.

Money isn't everything. This is usually said when we think people are putting too much emphasis on it. But, truthfully, it isn't! Being healthy, spiritually aware, and loved precede money in my life.

If God wanted me to have more, I would have more. If you instill this belief in your children, they may never aspire to lead more productive lives. This particular attitude asserts that people don't play an active part in their life's design. This means that your kids won't challenge themselves to *be* more and, therefore, *have* more. They'll spend a great portion of their lives waiting on someone—and not just God—to make their lives better, more enriched, and more fulfilling.

Everybody ain't gonna be rich. This is true, but why do we have to be the "ain't gots" all the time?

The poorer I am, the more God blesses me. I don't esteem a God who wants me to be poor. Some of us are teaching our kids to believe that they have to live in poverty. They don't. Some even hold on to a belief that suffering is good for the soul, and so in some way we may believe that God will reward us for being poor.

If I don't have it, I can't blow it. This is another dysfunction that floats around in our community. Perhaps you believe this because you had role models who were frivolous spenders and you never had a decent meal because of it. The key is to teach management and budgeting skills.

I don't need retirement, I'll live off my Social Security. You'll probably need more money to live on once you retire than you do now. You may have more health concerns, more debt, and so forth. Let's teach our kids to plan for their retirement now! Today! Then maybe they won't have to work right up until their retirement day.

A Li'l Somethin'

Use everyday occurrences to educate your kids about money. If your child rushes in and tells you that the team has decided to wear a different brand of sneaker this year, don't just shell out the money and dismiss the kid. Use this opportunity to talk about how he can come up with the money. Let him know that your help may not necessarily mean you'll foot the entire bill, either.

If your toddler reaches for a low-fat treat at the store, ask her if she has any money. Then notice the look on her face. She may be confused at first, but if this behavior is repeated enough, the child will remember to bring her coins the next time you announce you're going to the grocery store. And when she reaches for that treat and you ask your question, she'll pull out the money. She will have learned that goods cost money and that Dad or Mom will not buy her everything she wants, even if they can afford it.

Needs Versus Wants

The first thing every child needs to understand is the difference between needs and wants. When kids are young, they think everything is a need. They throw tantrums when they can't get their way. As they get older, they start to learn the difference between the two. It's your job to make sure they know the difference sooner rather than later.

Sit your kids down and talk about the necessities of life—food, water, shelter, love, and affection. Help them understand that it's likely they already have everything they need. Then explain that everything else falls into the category of wants and preferences, things to help make life more enjoyable. To *need* means to be without something essential to our existence or to our purposes. To *want* means to desire something that would supply pleasure.

You should also explain what I like to call "sanity money," funds to keep you from jumping off a cliff—money you use to have fun: for movies, massages, or long drives to the country. Let your kids decide how to spend their sanity money. If they enjoy music, they may choose to invest in a *Best of Barney* CD rather than a Verdi book or the latest Disney video. Don't judge how they spend sanity money (unless they violate rules) or you'll drive them crazy!

Ask your kids to define wants and needs. Have ready the handy definition above, but don't share it until after you've discussed their point of view. Share your definition, and then have a discussion about your respective definitions.

By now you've noticed that I continue to encourage dialogue between parents and kids. The easier it is for your kids to talk to you, the more you'll be able to teach them about money—and anything else, for that matter. Since we're talking about younger children, remember that you will have to find creative ways to hold their attention.

Explain to your kids the difference between the two concepts, and you are off to a good start. A good exercise is to sit down and pull out a sheet of paper with a "needs" and a "wants" column, as below.

NEEDS   WANTS

_____   _____

_____   _____

_____   _____

_____   _____

_____   _____

Make this a joint effort between you and your kids. Don't send them off to do this assignment on their own, especially if they can't write yet. Remember, talking about money is a *good* thing—no matter what has been drilled into your head. The more opportunities you seize to educate your children, the better.

Once you get your lists compiled, open up the discussion to explanations for answers. Remember, you want to be the model of the behavior you wish your child to exhibit. Avoid judging your child's answer: "That's not a need, stupid!" or "Oh, so movies are a need, huh?" Just let her finish her list and then start the conversation by saying something like "Okay, I'll start since this game was my idea. Now, I put a car as a need because Mom has to get to work, her job is thirty miles away, and no bus runs outside the city limits. What about you? Tell me about one of your needs and wants."

In this scenario you have set the tone for what should be an interesting, nonjudgmental conversation. Remember, no matter how tempting it is to shoot down her answer, don't. Instead, if your daughter says something that appears absurd to you (like she desperately needs a Kiana toy), simply ask her to support her answer. This way you are encouraging open communication and finding out a little bit more about her thinking patterns.

Teaching Kids Where Money Comes From

Unless you tell kids where money comes from, they won't know. They'll think when they get older that as long as they have checks, they have money. So the first lesson kids must learn is that you get money from working—period. Somebody worked for that paycheck. Teach them that they have food and shelter because you work. Take your toddlers to your job and explain what goes on there and that you are paid to do what you do.

Sir Charles—a Role Model?

Charles Barkley boldly announced a few years ago, "I am not a role model." Well, I think Charles was trying to convey that parents should strive to be the individuals kids emulate and aspire to be like, at least in part. That's what Charles was saying. But guess what, Charles? You *are* a role model even if you don't want to be. You didn't sign up for it, but you are. Kids *and* adults look up to you.

Likewise, your kids will, in many cases, follow in your footsteps. If we rush out to buy the latest car every time the design is changed, why shouldn't our kids kick this year's Nintendo aside and ask for the newest model? If we announce that we are going to the store to get a pair of gloves and also we buy a new leather coat and six pairs of shoes, why should we think that our kids won't do the same?

If our kids are polar opposites of us, it's because they've rejected us as role models. And this does happen. My parents had some behavior patterns that I rejected, and I'm sure you can say the same, right? So steering your children's money education is not so much about supervision as it is about watching your own step!

PEOPLE OUR KIDS LOOK UP TO

Hero worship may be a sign of a poverty-minded individual so we must step in and intervene as early as possible when we see our kids idolizing or worshiping people. And this is not limited to the Michael Jordans, Sheryl Swoopes, or Oprah Winfreys of the world, either. Sometimes kids worship common folk like ministers, teachers, and coaches. There is a difference between admiring and worshiping. To *admire* someone is to appreciate their particular talent, skill, or beauty. I admired my mother for going back to school at age forty. To *worship* means to revere, to esteem in the highest manner. If your kids begin to talk about people as though they are infallible and untouchable, look out. They could be hero worshipers. I'm no psychologist, but generally people who delight in idolizing have severe self-esteem issues. Based on everything I've read, it's perfectly normal to admire someone, famous or not, because it teaches a valuable social skill: appreciating someone else's gifts. Just make sure that your kid doesn't transform before your eyes into someone else—someone he idolizes.

The Kids Will Hear

Please be careful what you say around your kids about your job, coworkers, employees, employers, and so forth. You don't want them to be cynics before they even enter the working world. Even if you've had a bad day and you want to talk to your Honey about it, take it to your bedroom or some other private area.

And Now a Word from Our Sponsors: The Effects of Advertising

Although you may feel that you've cornered the market on teaching your kids, they are growing up in a world completely different from the one you grew up in. For instance, television is full of gimmicks and campaigns designed to get our hard-earned dollars. So what do we do when our kids ask for a $200 pair of sneakers or a $30 pair of underwear? Some of us dole out the money and never blink. And when we do, what message are we giving our kids?

Last year advertisers spent millions of dollars to attract African-American consumers. If you don't think the world has changed, check out this chart.

Item	1966 Price	1996 Price
Pair of sneakers	$20.00	$125.00
Pair of jeans	$15.00	$75.00
Single pair silk underwear	$4.00	$24.00
Loaf of bread	.15	$1.10

What can we do to curb the effects of advertising on our kids? For starters, stop letting your kids watch so much TV. If you don't believe you can do this (because you work long hours) or are not willing to (because you watch a lot yourself), at least discuss advertising with your kids. Let's say that Jackie Joyner-Kersee appears on television promoting a sports drink. Instead of sitting on the sofa and absorbing the message, call a time-out and ask your kids something like this: "Hey, Janessa. If I took you to the store right now and asked you to pick up something for the family to drink after workouts, what would you choose?" If she says the product that Jackie was just endorsing, ask her why.

Michael Jordan's fragrance came on the market and immediately made enormous grosses. Why? Because of several factors: (1) it's a nice fragrance, (2) people like Mike, (3) people are still trying to *be* like Mike, and (4) every time you turned around, there was a commercial, billboard, or some other form of advertising trying to get you to do one thing—try it or buy it. That is the purpose of advertising: trial or commitment.

Talking to our kids about consumer decisions has never been more crucial. All of us have fallen prey to advertising at one time or another. Have you ever been watching television when all of a sudden a pizza commercial came on, showing the pie fresh out of the oven, dripping with cheese? You had finished dinner less than two hours prior, but you still reached for the phone and dialed that easy-to-remember number while singing that catchy little tune, didn't you? Now, were you actually hungry? Probably not. Are you that crazy about pizza? Probably not. But something about the advertising appealed to your senses. Either it was the setting of the advertising (perhaps a group of friends sitting around having a good time) or it was the food itself that enticed you. Something made you make a conscious decision to support the advertiser.

Why do you think companies sometimes choose celebrities instead of regular people to appear in their commercials? To look as if they're supporting their products, especially when they're pushing a product geared toward blacks? To get us to order the pizza! Advertisers have studied our habits and our attitudes. They basically believe that we are hero worshipers and are motivated to keep up with the Joneses of the world.

Advertisers are even more clever when it comes to our kids. They know how much black children want to identify with winners and celebrities, so they use famous voices to reach our kids. I'm almost insulted at how hard advertisers work to get our dollars. They think our kids are more impressionable or that they're not getting any message intervention at home. They believe our kids will fall hook, line, and sinker for their media messages.

A professor at Texas A & M University, James McNeal, says that kids begin to express preferences by their third birthday, mostly surrounding toy decisions. Three years old! A three-year-old is not going to know the difference between a pair of Filas and Pay Less specials. But we must avoid forcing our children to get caught up in the mania of brand-name madness. A prime example is the hysteria surrounding the Tickle Me Elmo dolls during the 1996 Christmas holidays. I heard on the radio that people were running around like crazy trying to find these little dolls. And for what? For one-, two-, and three-year-olds? I guarantee you they wouldn't know the difference if you got them a look-alike or something totally different. My two-year-old niece did not ask her father for this fuzzy red animal with the egg-yolk-sized eyes, but my brother bought her one anyway because *he* had gotten caught up in the marketing glitz and glamour. His daughter ended up hating the doll—it scared her.

Do you see what I mean about us turning our kids into monsters? Eventually our kids tend to place emphasis on the things *we* emphasize as parents. What's ironic is that when our kids emulate our bad habits we get angry and say "I don't know where she got that from." Look in the mirror.

Recently, I drove through an ethnic section of Los Angeles and noticed several billboards advertising designer clothes—Tommy Hilfiger, Calvin Klein. Pretty soon I saw kids walking down the boulevard with "Tommy" splattered across their chests. *Voilà!* Mission accomplished.

Next time you and your kids are watching television together, talk about the ads. This is a good way to get into your child's mind and learn how he thinks and responds to advertising messages.

Drugs and Gangs

It's sad that I have to address this in a section about kids five years old and younger, but that's our reality today. Yes, drugs and gangs have been around since the beginning of time but not to the degree that they invade our communities today. Contemporary drug dealers are not as discreet as they were twenty years ago. I was horrified the day my little brother, who's ten years younger than I, called me while I was away in college and told me his friend had been propositioned to sell drugs. My reaction? I thought the mother should get him out of that school. Mind you this was the same school I had gone to, the same school my two older brothers and sister had gone to. But this school, which was rich in tradition and cultural identity, was now a stomping ground for some major drug dealing.

Although it wasn't a member of my family, I sat on the other end of the phone frantic. My brother calmly explained that this was the '90s. He was used to it. He even said that once *he'd* been asked to make a delivery. "I told 'em, 'Naw, man, that ain't me,' and walked off," he explained. And here was a five-year-old, being offered a $300-a-day job! In my brother's case it wasn't like he was going home to filet mignon every night, but, thankfully, my father was a hardworking man and had done a good job of instilling solid values in us. Let's face it, this is what our kids are up against.

Several months ago I saw an interview with a well-known African-American actor. The interviewer asked if he was anxious about the current climate that most African-American children are facing in school. He said, "Oh, no, I'm not worried about that. My daughter's in private school." My mouth flung open, and my lips hit my lap. Hel-loooo! And?

Just in case you are one of those naive sisters or brothers who thinks that your neighborhood, school district, or income bracket will protect you and your kids from the evils of this world, let me be the one to give you an earnest wake-up call. Please, for your kids' sake, be prepared. A kid looking for fast cash needn't look further than the schoolyard to find a chunk of loot that would choke Godzilla. We have to be aware of how enticing the lure of drugs is to black kids regardless of their background or parents' occupation. Dealers don't care who your mother or father is. Rich and privileged kids are selling drugs, as are inner-city youths, although the media would have us believe that only a certain portion of the population sells drugs. So don't think your kid is immune to life as a drug dealer because she attends a private school and is in the debate club.

> Parents must act as filters for the negative depictions that the media and the dominant society perpetrate.

Joe Louis's mother gave him $50 to pay for violin lessons. Know what he did? He rented a locker at Brewer East Side Gymnasium in Detroit and started training as a boxer.

What Can You Teach a Child at This Age?

Is it realistic to think that we can really raise kids to be financially responsible in an instant-gratification, ego-centered, brand-name-is-better, and mo' money world? You bet! But we have to start early, and we have to be consistent. Don't expect to tighten the rules overnight on a twelve-year-old who has been allowed to have his way from the time he got home from the hospital. How can you get angry with a child who only behaves the way he's been trained to? A few weeks ago I had Brittany clipping the coupons from the day's mail. She sat on the floor just cutting away while I was in the kitchen cooking. Suddenly she exclaimed, "Mom, you will not believe this! Mr. Gonzola's wants $11.99 for this supreme pizza when I just saw the same pizza on Little Caesar's sheet for $9.99! Are they crazy or what?" I just smiled and said, "Humph, imagine that, baby." That exchange is the result of sitting down with her one time and talking her through coupons when she was six and a half. I went through nearly fifty coupons, and then we discussed them, compared them, talked about their contents, and everything. And it was fun, so don't think this has to be a chore.

This is no easy task, and you are in for the time of your life. Get ready for resistance, pouty faces, a thousand "whys," and puffy eyes because you will get this and much more. You should never personalize their words. They still love you, and they want to know that you love them. But guess what? After the smoke clears and the eyes dry and they apologize for saying that they hate you, you will have given your child a truly great gift . . . and your wallet will be forever grateful that you did.

Believe it or not, kids who are younger than three years old know what money is. They don't know all that it does, but they recognize it as an exchange medium. Kids ages two to five are concerned with getting—and then getting some more. They understand spending above everything else. It's up to us to help them grasp earning and saving.

Take advantage of teaching them whatever they can understand even if it's only money identification. Remember that kids learn through play. They have reasonably short attention spans, so they need stimulation. When you get ready to teach them a skill, say something like "Let's play a really fun game, okay?" Don't say, "Sit down, son. I want to teach you a very important life skill." Won't work.

Recently I took my twenty-month-old niece, Taylor, to the gym with me. As we were leaving the gym, we passed a section full of vending machines. Hearing me jingle the change in my shorts pocket, she said, "I want some money." First I smiled and told her to ask by saying, "Auntie, may I have some money, please?" I figured that since children this age have no concept of begging, I would comply. I handed her a quarter and was curious to see what she would do with it.

She headed to a vending machine. She searched for a slot to stick her quarter in and began pushing selections. She had no idea that drinks don't cost twenty-five cents, but obviously she'd seen someone walk up to a vending machine, put money in, and get something out. So what can Taylor learn at twenty months? She can learn what a penny, nickel, dime, quarter, or even a dollar looks like. That's a great start. She'll be ahead of the game when it's time to count money.

By the way, when Taylor's Pa-Pa (my father) gives her a five-dollar bill, she always smiles and says, "Thank you, Pa-Pa." Please teach your kids to express gratitude no matter what the gift, large or small! At one of my brother's basketball games, I witnessed something that we can probably all identify with: A young boy—I'd say around thirteen or fourteen—walked up to a gentleman whom I assumed was his father. The boy asked for concession stand money. The man handed him a couple of dollars. The boy proceeded to express his dissatisfaction with the amount of money he'd been given. While the boy grimaced, frowned, and mumbled, the man pulled out a five-dollar bill. The boy gave the man the original bills, snatched the five, and took off toward the concession stand. No "thank you." No other signs of gratitude—no smile, no hug. Nothing.

It took all I had not to say something to the boy and the man separately. It was really none of my business, but this kind of blatant disrespect and lack of appreciation really gets to me. Are you raising or have you raised an unappreciative child? In my opinion, everything starts at home. If you teach your children to say thank you, they will. And if you yourself say thank you—to them and others—they'll be especially conscientious in this area.

SEVEN BIGGEST MONEY NO-NOS FOR BLACK PARENTS

1. **Don't equate money with love.** For example, if your child asks, "Mommy, do you love me?" don't answer, "Of course I do. I bought you that fire truck, didn't I?"
2. **Don't offer money when you screw up.** Let's say you cancel for the third time in three weeks. Don't say, "Hey, how 'bout I getcha that doll you've been wanting."
3. **Don't use money as a one-upsperson ploy.** Let's say your kids think your spouse is too strict with money. In an effort to make your spouse be the bad one, then, you let your kids know that your money is abundant, and whenever they want some, they can just ask for it.
4. **Don't use money as a tool to get your kids to like you, prefer you, or value you.** Let's say your kids don't particularly care for you, or to be around you (money is the least of your worries if you have this problem), so you start buying them everything they ask for as well as a few things they haven't even thought about. They may *tolerate* you as long as

you're shelling out the dough, but don't confuse this situational politeness for "like" or love.

5. **Don't ever say, "Here, take it, and just leave me alone."** Money doesn't equal time. I've heard of many kids who resent their parents for handing them money when what they really wanted (and were asking for) was their time and attention.

6. **Don't ever give your son more money than your daughter just because he's a boy.** No elaboration necessary.

7. **Don't ever replace money that a child has lost.** Covering your child's mistake may make him stop crying momentarily, but it won't teach him the value of money or responsible behavior.

Kidz Play: Money Games

THE NAME GAME

Objective: to teach the names of coins. Can be varied for older kids.

Tools: twelve 3-by-5 index cards, two pennies, two nickels, two dimes, two quarters, two half-dollars, two dollar coins, three markers (each a different color), tape, and patience.

Method: Take six cards and tape one of each coin to the center of each card. Print clearly underneath the denomination of the money. Take the other six cards and tape the coins on them, but this time don't write the denomination underneath it.

Stand in front of your child and show the first set of cards several times. Show the card and then say the coin's name. Have your child repeat this after you. Go through the process again, but this time only your child should identify it. Once you've done this several times, use the second set and see how well your child does in identifying the coins.

Lessons: money identification and responsibility (by being your helper at the end and putting the money and cards away).

For older kids, allow them to see only the cards without the denominations on them and tell you how much each is worth.

Remember to reward after each correct answer—a high five, hug, smile, cartwheel, and so forth. Children get very excited when you get excited, and they'll be extremely eager to learn the next task.

PHOTO FUN

Objective: to identify coins.

Tools: several pennies, nickels, dimes, and quarters, and photos of different family members.

Method: Place your photos in a line on the floor or on a table. Place the coins on the table in no particular order. Ask your child to give each family member (there may be more than one person in a picture) one of the coins. You might say, for instance, "Let's say Aunt Lucille has a birthday coming up, and she's always wanted a nickel. Let's give her a nickel." Let your child look around for a nickel and give it to the appropriate relative. When the game is finished, tell your child that you are going to put the photos away again in a safe place—either in a box or in a frame, wherever they came from. Let him follow and watch, then tell him that the two of you need to find a safe place for the money as well. Ask him for suggestions.

Lessons: coin identification and responsibility. This will also help him understand later that banks are another safe place to put money.

Kitchen Fun

Objective: to learn counting.

Tools: any number of small kitchen appliances— spoons (no forks or knives), bowls, cups, or different vegetables and fruits.

Method: If you're artistically inclined, you may want to draw the items on index cards and proceed as in the first game. If not, you can simply arrange all the items in a pile and hold them up one by one, repeating the name of each and having your child repeat after you. Once you've done this a few times, you hold up each item and have your child identify it. Don't forget to praise.

Lessons: mathematics and identification of household items. Although you may not see the immediate correlation with money, counting is essential to developing money skills.

This game can be upgraded for older kids and teenagers by including uses, measuring, and cooking. Cooking is also an excellent tool for teaching money skills because it utilizes both time and measurements.

How Many Are There?

Objective: to identify coins and learn to divide—how many smaller denominations of coins are in the larger ones.

Tools: two quarters, five dimes, ten nickels, and ten pennies, an 8½-by-11 sheet of paper, and a marker.

Method: Using the marker, draw an equals symbol (=) in the middle of the sheet. Place the coins before your child and show her how many different ways money can be divided to equal a particular amount. To start, take a nickel and place it on one side of the equals sign. Place five pennies on the other side. Count the pennies and explain to the child that one nickel is the same as five pennies. Increase the denominations and variations until you get to fifty cents.

Lessons: fast recognition of how change is made, and children begin to understand that coins are interchangeable and that one nickel is just as good as five pennies.

As the child gets older, use larger bills and more coins.

Money Bingo

Objective: to identify coins.

Tools: for each child participating, a 5-by-7 card with boxes drawn as on a bingo card and with random drawings of pennies, nickels, dimes, quarters, half-dollars, and dollar coins in the boxes, plus markers.

Method: Call out the names of coins until someone has gotten five coins in a diagonal, horizontal, or vertical configuration.

Lessons: listening, attention to details, and familiarity with coins.

LET'S GO SHOPPING

Objective: to match prices with items.

Tools: variety of household items.

Method: Place blank price tags on a few items around the house. Have your child write what he thinks the retail price is for each item. You will have a master list with real prices. Match your list with what your child writes on tags. Discuss afterward.

Lesson: the value of commodities.

NEEDS VERSUS WANTS

Objective: to learn the difference between needing and wanting.

Tools: variety of household and personal items.

Method: Place a few items in front of your child and ask her to identify them as needs or wants.

Lesson: We own many things because we want them, not because we need them.

TREASURE HUNT

Objective: to steer kids away from their desire for instant gratification.

Tools: fruit basket with a variety—bananas, apples, pears, and so forth.

Method: Hide each piece of fruit in a different area in your home and challenge your child to find each fruit to complete the basket, the treasure. Give an appropriate reward—not money.

Lesson: patience and deferred gratification.

CHORES FOR PRESCHOOLERS

Chores should start as soon as a child can walk. A child who can walk probably has pretty good motor skills. Although you shouldn't expect your one-year-old to pull up a high chair and go after the dinner dishes, you certainly can require him to pick up his toys and put them in the toy box. But first you will have to show him how. It usually isn't very effective to provide a lengthy explanation to a toddler. If you want him to do something, remember to *show and tell*. Even if he seems uninterested at first, you should say, "Trevor, help Dad pick up your blocks," while putting them in the bin yourself. Pretty soon he will start imitating you. Remember to praise by thanking, smiling, hugging, high-fiving, or clapping when the task is complete.

In case you're wondering what a two-year-old can do, check out these suggestions:

Daddy's/Mom's little helper: cleaning the garage. Tell your toddler to pick up the trash and put it in the big green bag, that that's *her* job.

Toy pickup: Don't let that kid get away with leaving toys strewn around the house. Make putting toys in the toy box a game.

Remember, for younger kids you have to make it fun.

When Games Should End

During a money game or lesson, I can always tell when the vacancy or For Rent sign is flashing across my

---

daughter's forehead and it's time to stop the game. She drifts and floats away right before my eyes. With any of the games, when your young child starts wandering off, it's time to stop. Use such phrases as "Okay, boys and girls, that's the end of our show for today. We'll see you next time." Avoid saying such things as "Looky here, you sit your little butt down and pay attention. This is important." And don't grab up the cards and put them away yourself. Instead, encourage your kids to help you find a special place for them.

PIGGY BANKS

When your child is a preschooler, it is a good time to get a bank. I'll assume that someone decided to make piggy banks because of the pig's expansive middle, but you can use anything to make a bank. And let's be sensible. There's no need to rush out to purchase them. You can role-model creativity and money smarts by making them out of something you have at home, such as a margarine container or Cool Whip–type bowl. Cut a slit in the top and *voilà*! Instant banking. Your child can decorate the container, putting on it his name, athletic number, and so forth.

You should make several banks, each with its own label. The chief objective is to make sure you have a container for the "NSLTEC" concepts:

- **N**ow or Spending: funds to be used on immediate wants and needs such as movies and other recreational activities.
- **S**hort-term Saving: funds your child plans to use for

an event or item to be purchased within the next six months.

- **Long-term Saving:** funds to be used for a long-term project, maybe a birthday or another holiday purchase or for that special play date trip to the zoo.
- **Taxes:** self-explanatory, but kids need to contribute to this jar each time they are paid so they get accustomed to how much money they *really* have for spending.
- **Extra Bank:** funds to be used for whatever you and your child decide, such as charity, emergency funds, and gift planning.
- **College Bank:** to be used for this expected activity. If your child has a pennant, T-shirt, or cap from a college, have her set it up next to the bank. Talk to your child about the kinds of things she may need once she gets to college.

Remember that in all instances of spending saved money, the purchase or activity cannot conflict with family values.

Helpful Hints for Working with Toddlers and Preschoolers

- Dress up in funny costumes (tell 'em you're the *Sesame Street* Money Fairy).
- Speak in funny voices, their favorite comic strip or animated friends.
- Vary your voice. Go shrill and get low.
- Blindfold yourself if the game will allow.
- Invite one of their favorite stuffed friends to watch.
- Play outdoors.

- Watch to make sure they don't swallow coins.
- Collect all coins after using them in a game.

> Warning! Children at this age are very curious, but, more important, they tend to put things in their mouths. Please be careful.

THE WONDER YEARS

The Sassy Sixes,
Saucy Sevens,
Eager Eights . . .

Talking to Kids About Money
So That They'll Listen

If you want to photocopy a section of this book to hang up on the wall as a reminder, this is it.

The way you talk to your kids and others about money will put a lasting imprint on their minds and in their hearts, so be careful. This is not an area to take lightly. Your kids have already been listening to you talk about money (whether you know it or not)—to creditors, friends, family, coworkers, the newspaper girl/boy, and so forth. They've heard you have numerous conversations about that green, copper, and silver stuff, and they've listened well.

There's a good chance that when you start Money 101 with your six-year-old, she'll be able to tell you a few things, too—such as she noticed that $50 bill in your wallet at the grocery store, so why did you say you didn't have any money? I don't lie about money, especially to my daughter. You should consider this policy as well. If Brittany asks for something and I don't want her to have it, I say no. Sometimes the reason is that we don't buy cereals with tons of sugar in them. Sometimes it's that whatever she wants isn't in the budget. She's seven, and she understands this after a year in Money 202. She's not a freshie anymore. Now she approaches a purchase or activity in one of two ways: "Mom, is this in our budget?" or "Mom, I'm going to get this with my allowance next month." Her financial IQ is much higher than mine was at her age, and it's because she's being taught. She already talks about planning and saving, checkbooks and credit cards, debt and taxes. And what I love is that she's curious. She's not intimidated. She wants to learn more.

Kids around this age are also tuning into your conversations with your spouse and others about money. Plus, they have their own preconceived notions about it, how you feel about it, and its role in your household. If kids constantly hear you and your spouse bicker about how tight money is, they may wonder why there's such a shortage of the stuff and why their parents get so angry when they talk about it. They may take it a little further and say if the stuff makes their parents that angry, then they'll make sure (1) they never have any to fight about, (2) when their significant other gets angry about it, that they make concessions so there isn't a fight, or (3) that they'll kill themselves working so they'll always have plenty of money (but no life). We don't want our kids to take any of these positions, do we? I sure hope not. These are not healthy relationships with one of the most valuable assets available to us.

Be Honest in Your Responses

Remember how crazy it drove you when your parents said, "We'll see," when you asked to go somewhere or wanted something? Sometimes they granted our requests, and sometimes they didn't. As a six-year-old, I couldn't help but wonder whether my mom really intended to do what I'd requested or if she was just trying to make me suffer.

Parents, if you know that you are not going to do something, say no. Don't delay the inevitable. You're not being 100 percent honest, a pattern we don't want our kids to develop.

At the same time, if you truly are unsure about something, say so. Tell your kids that you haven't thought it through yet and that you will get back to them later. Remember, though, that kids' perception of time often differs from ours. *Later* may mean two hours to us, but to them it's more like ten minutes. Make the lapse a reasonable span of time. Don't stall just because you have the power. Remember that when you do this, you are role-modeling behaviors that aren't appropriate.

Seven Laws of Black Money Success

Below are a few values that your six- through twelve-year-olds can definitely understand.

1. **Pay yourself first.** When I get an advance from a publisher, I discuss it with Brittany—not necessarily the amount, but I tell her I'm about to be paid to write a book. She immediately gets excited and asks what "we" are going to do with the money. After I finish teasing her about being so "plural" with *my* advance, I tell her that I'm going to pay me and then put some away for tax planning. Then I tell her that authors have to be their own budgeters because they get paid only when they write a book.

The wealthy believe in the "pay me first" rule. You worked for the money, so why shouldn't you be the first to reap the benefits? Teach your kids to treat themselves for working hard.

2. **Give yourself an allowance.** An allowance is money that you take out of your earnings for recreation or something special for yourself. Let your kids know that if they manage their money—even if it's fifty cents a week—they'll always have a stash they can count on.

3. **Set goals.** Teach them that the way to success or

achievement is through consistent goal setting. Teach them that goals must be clear, specific, measurable, and stretch them as a person. Talk to them about each of these criteria.

4. **Review your goals and progress at least twice a year.** Keep the word *goals* as part of your everyday household lingo. Our kids need to understand how empowering this process is.

5. **Don't beat yourself up (too long) over money mistakes.** If your child makes an error such as giving the clerk too much money or not getting the correct change, don't berate or embarrass her. Instead, calmly ask her what she thinks she should do. If it involves going back to talk to a clerk, accompany her. Don't take over—that can be demoralizing. The clerk will notice that you're with the child and will probably be patient as the child explains what happened.

6. **Increase your capacity for risk.** Risk is an interesting concept to teach kids at this age because they're usually pretty scared of losing. Try an exercise or game such as the one Brittany and I use. We'll play a game of checkers, and I'll issue a challenge: If you beat me in this game, you get to stay up an extra thirty minutes. If you lose, you have to go to bed thirty minutes earlier. At first their eyes may get as big as saucers at the prospect of losing, but when they win, they understand that by playing they have an equal chance of feeling good or disappointed. That's what risk is. You never know the outcome; you just step out on faith.

7. **Talk to your children about faith.** Talk to your children about believing in something that maybe they

can't see or touch. It's an important concept to discuss. Give the chair example: When they go to school and select a seat, do they ask the chair if it will support their body, or do they just position their body and have faith that the chair will be there?

The Biggest Mistakes African-American Parents Make with Their Children

Showering them with gifts: What is a reasonable gift for your six-year-old's birthday? What message are you sending or what expectations are you setting up by giving a child a video game plus ten pairs of pants plus a set of golf clubs *and* a trip to Chuck E Cheese? Even if you have gobs of money, exercise some restraint and discretion. We sometimes give gifts for our *own* gratification—to see the smile on our child's face. Well, this year for Christmas I bought Brittany some hiking boots and her first watch. That's it! She loves them both. Your kids will appreciate any gift you give them. Just don't set them or yourself up to be disappointed. Believe me, if you give your child ten gifts for his birthday this year, he'll wonder what's gotten into you if he gets only one the following year.

Giving money to kids without requiring them to earn it: This means giving an allowance of $20 a week when this girl's room is never clean, she brings home lousy grades (which is not to be confused with paying kids to get good grades—we'll talk about that later), or she talks back.

Teaching kids that money equals success: This refers to making such comments as "Mr. Green's got it going on, son. He makes $125,000 a year."

Giving kids the impression that money is the ultimate goal: You say, "Annette, if I could just make $50,000, I'd be set." The message a child may get is that money equals happiness or that it erases all our other problems.

Saying "Do as I say": The implication is "Do as I say, and not as I do." My mother said it, and I always thought (but never said it, of course), "If you think it's such a good idea for me to do, why aren't you doing it?" Don't talk a talk vastly different from your walk. It's hypocritical and it confuses your kids.

Giving the impression that "stuff equals love": Ooooh, this is a big one for us. Some of us really believe that our kids' love for us goes through the ceiling when we give them more things, toys, and so forth. Wrong! In fact, kids' *enthusiasm* may soar but their *love* is unchanged by gifts. Kids need love and attention more than stuff. Remember this and you'll save yourself a lot of money in the short and long run.

Not using every opportunity to teach them about money: Instead of yelling at your daughter when she asks you for more money after blowing her allowance, use this opportunity to teach her about budgeting. Don't just yell and then give her the money anyway.

Not discussing money: Some kids never have a *discussion* with their parents about money—it's always a one-sided communication. They ask, and the parents say either yes or no. End of story. This is a big mistake. We cripple our kids when we refuse to discuss money with them.

Not letting them experience money: You can't manage what you don't have. So why get angry with your eight-year-old when he blows his birthday money in one day? You have done nothing to improve his money management skills. Give him a weekly allowance so he can practice and become comfortable with it.

Assuming they understand how money works: Kids begin to see that money is a medium of exchange. They see you give it to the checkout person to get groceries or purchase other items. Don't let them assume that this is money's only function. Money has different levels of use. We pay taxes so that we can have police and fire departments. Money covers these and many other services.

Fighting about money in front of them without any explanations: Your kids come home from school every day and hear you on the phone fighting with someone about money: who should have paid what, who didn't pay what, and how you're not going to keep paying the phone bill. This kind of dialogue has a profound impact on a child, so if you don't want your child in "grown folks' business," as some of us have told our children, then keep your business a little quieter. Speak when your children aren't around or at least offer them some explanation as to why the discussion about money was so heated.

Taking their money away from them: Let's say your nine-year-old daughter earns money by mowing a neighbor's lawn. You go to her and insist that she give you all her money. What do you think her reaction will be? She may give it to you, but she'll resent the "you know what" out of you. Besides her resentment, you are teaching her a horrible lesson: It's okay for authority figures to bully subordinates. If you would like your daughter to help with household expenses, explain *up front* that one of the objectives of her employment is to help out with expenses. Don't let her take the job with the expectation that she can keep whatever she earns, and then *wham!* you tell her that all along you wanted her money. This also implies that she is not responsible enough to hold her own money. It's deceitful, and it cultivates an environment of dishonesty and mistrust—not just for you and your daughter in the present but also for her in the long term.

The Biggest Mistakes
Kids Make with Money

Overextending themselves: They learn this from us. If we say that we're going to the grocery store for a gallon of milk and come back with additional impulse items, what's a kid to think?

Borrowing from friends: Explain to your kids that money is an important resource and that you should be careful as to whom you borrow it from and why you're borrowing.

Not being satisfied with what they have: They also learn this from us. It seems that sometimes we want what eludes us. We are never quite satisfied with what we have, and if we go even deeper, sometimes we are not satisfied with who we are. Contentment appears to be light-years away from many black folks. Consequently, our kids are always chasing something—a bigger car, shinier jewelry, or a louder stereo. Let's teach them to strive for greater inner peace instead of outer satisfaction.

Lending money: While we may want our children to share their resources, we certainly don't want them to do so without understanding the lending process. Lending means that the party receiving the money will pay it back; otherwise, your child is *giving* money away. While there's nothing wrong with giving someone money, be sure your child understands the difference between the two before parting with the money.

Not understanding the *perceived* power of money in the black community: This addresses a deep-seated psychological issue within the black culture: the notion that people with money are automatically "better" than those who have none or less of it. We must teach our kids that their value as people has absolutely nothing to do with the size of their bank account. Too many of our kids are equating their worth with their purchasing power.

Stashing all their money: Frugality to the nth degree makes kids little misers, and we don't want to raise misers. Encourage your kids to buy themselves something with their money, even if it's a puzzle or a video.

Responsibility, Accountability, and Budgeting

This is one of the most critical sections in the book. First, let's define responsibility.

> Responsibility: the ability to respond favorably in any given situation; to take care of something.

Young kids will get the concept if you talk about it again and again. Explain to your child that taking his books to school is a responsibility, something he is in charge of. Try the property approach:

"Jimmy, who sleeps in your bed?"

"I do."

"So who is in charge of making your bed?"

"I am."

"That's what I mean about responsibility, Jimmy. You take care of things that are yours."

The same is true when you start talking about chores. Create a sense of ownership. Kids like that. If the garage is her area, then call it hers when you talk about it: "How's your garage doing, Katy?" or "Boy, your garage has sure been looking great these days!" She'll smile and stick her chest out. Cultivate pride and ownership.

Accountability: the act of owning one's actions and behaviors.

Example: Dinner is set for 6:00 P.M. Your son is running late because he is out riding with a buddy from tennis practice. Instead of calling you to tell you he will arrive late, he waltzes in and simply says that it wasn't his fault, he wasn't driving. Your job is to get your son to see that the proper behavior would have been to extend you and the rest of the family a courtesy call.

Budgeting: how money travels in and out of your household.

Is seven years old too early to talk about budgets? Not at all. To give a child this young a sense of how budgets work, put him in charge. Let's say your son has four action figures. You tell him that you've bought four apples and four oranges for his crew and that he needs to make sure that each figure has enough to eat. Your son will probably give each figure one apple and one orange, thereby budgeting his food.

After he explains what he has done, you take the floor. Tell him that each week there are things that must be done—grocery shopping, paying bills, and so forth. Explain that you get only one paycheck, and that this paycheck has to be spread around. Not only will he begin to get a better idea of what budgeting is, he'll begin to understand how important your role is to the family unit.

Budgets change, of course. Explain to your older kids the difference between fixed and variable expenses. Fixed expenses are those items in your family finances that don't change—or at least not regularly—such as the mortgage, car payments, tithing or monthly charitable donations, electricity, and maybe monthly club dues. Variable expenses are those items that change or that come and go, such as vacations, gifts, and entertainment.

Once your kids understand the difference, give them a little test for fun. List a few items and ask them to put an F or V beside the word. Remember to make it fun. Also open up a discussion about why budgets change—unemployment, a new baby, unexpected occurrences.

Chores

A great place to start when you want to instill responsibility and accountability in your kids is to assign chores. Did your parents instill strict chore policies in your home when you were growing up? I remember when I was about nine years old, my brothers used to get up and mow the lawn every Saturday before they went to the gym to play basketball. I remember them getting up at the crack of dawn sometimes because they knew that Mom was not going to allow them to go anywhere before their jobs were done. Ten years later my little brother had to do one thing: wash dishes. And I remember thinking how lackadaisical he was about doing them. Sometimes they would sit in the kitchen sink for hours while he either talked on the phone or hung out with his friends after practice. He had no real sense of responsibility, not like his older brothers.

Chores are a great introduction to money skills because part of learning to manage money centers around responsibility and discipline. If our kids can master responsibility and discipline, half of the money battle is won. But first we must make a commitment to giving our children the gift of chores. And although they won't see them as a gift, that's what you're giving them—an opportunity to seize control over their financial futures.

Q. *I can't get my son to clean up his room for anything! Should I offer him money?*

A. Have you hit your head on a hard surface lately? Depending on your son's age, he should've already been taught that his room is part of his responsibility to the household. You work to provide food and shelter, and his job includes picking up after himself. No. Do not begin paying kids to do what they should be required to do as members of the family. But you might want to try cooperation versus confrontation.

In other words, marching into his room

late at night to confront him won't make either of you feel real good. Instead, open a discussion about it over breakfast and tell your son what you expect. You'll have to decide on the consequences based on what's important to your child. Privileges were a big thing in my home, so that always worked for my parents.

Here are a few ideas if you're stuck on finding chores: washing and folding laundry, doing the dishes, setting the table, clearing the table, dusting, washing the car, polishing doorknobs, vacuuming, loading and unloading the dishwasher, making a grocery list, taking out the trash, coupon clipping, newspaper recycling, sweeping and mopping, arranging scattered CDs and audio cassettes, organizing bookshelves, cleaning the attic or the garage, and doing lawn or yard work.

THE ART OF CHORE GIVING

As your kids get older, they probably will grumble and gripe about doing chores. If they don't, they're a special breed, and you're one of the lucky few. But don't let their antics get you down—it's their job, just as giving chores is yours.

The important thing about making chores work in your home is to give your kids some options. If I knew that I had to mop the kitchen floor 365 days a year, I'd eventually hate it with a passion. But if I knew that on some days of the year I could choose my chores, I'd have a better attitude.

A good idea is to make a chart and give your kids their "regular chores"—such as keeping their rooms tidy or taking out the garbage—but then add some flavor to the routine by either rotating chores among your kids or adding extra chores so they will feel as if they have some say in their misery. Also, rotating chores gives them an appreciation for different kinds of work and the work you do on a regular basis. Here's a sample chore chart for six- to twelve-year-olds.

Posted: Monday, May 4, 1998, at 9:30 A.M.

Person	*Chore*	*Due Date*
Kevin	Dinner dishes	After dinner, Mon. to Thur.
Jessica	Raking leaves	No later than Sun., 5:00 P.M.
Lourdis	Cleaning fridge	No later than Sat., 2:00 P.M.

Special Clause for Nine- to Twelve-Year-Olds: You may trade one of your specific chores for the following:

1. Hand-wash both vehicles, including interior vacuuming and so forth. *This must be done no later than 9 on Saturday morning.*
2. Clean out and organize the garage by Sunday at 5 P.M.
3. Wash the windows by Saturday at 5 P.M.

OVERWORKED?

One day I passed my daughter's room and noticed her sitting on the bed sulking. When I asked what was wrong, she proceeded to tell me that she felt she did all the work around the house. I sat next to her on the bed and asked her to tell me about all this work *she* supposedly did. "Cleaning my room and taking out the trash," she answered. I said that I'd like to share some of my jobs with her: cooking dinner, driving her to school, working, washing clothes, vacuuming, cleaning the bathroom, paying the bills, and taking care of her when she's sick. "Now do you still think *you* do all the work around here?" I asked. She didn't say a word (smart girl). With that, I rose from the bed and quietly left as she sat on the bed and watched me leave. I never heard *that* again!

PAYING FOR CHORES AND OTHER CHILD LABOR

It is strictly your choice whether you pay your child to do chores. If you decide to pay a child, it becomes a job, not a chore. Here is a sample of things you should *never* pay your children to do: be courteous; clean their rooms and other personal spaces; respect others; anything related to hygiene and personal development—brushing teeth, combing hair, bathing; putting things in their proper place around the house; their homework; to go to school or church; to pray; to eat; to do their extracurricular activities. Does that about cover it all? Never pay your kids to do something that you believe in your heart they should contribute freely.

What if you have a teenager and a toddler? Should you pay your fifteen-year-old to baby-sit her brother? Not always. Let's say you have a party you want to go to on Saturday, and that's the day your teenager usually goes out with her friends. If she's agreeable to staying home to allow you to go out and have a good time, then I say that offering a small monetary gift is a nice gesture. She won't expect the money, but she'll appreciate the offer and will probably accept it if she's smart! If you've done a good job, your kids know that caring for one another is something that is done out of love. Remind them that no one paid you to take care of them.

Hiring kids is another matter. Let's say you need the shed painted, and you don't really want to hire a professional. Should you consider kid labor? Of course. Announce to your kids that there's a job to be done and that they could make some extra money for a good job. You can type up an ad on your typewriter or word processor and post it on the refrigerator or wherever you put announcements.

> **WANTED:** Individuals to paint the toolshed. This job pays $1.25 an hour. Meet in the backyard no later than 10:00 A.M. on Saturday, October 17. Wear comfortable old clothes. Bring your own lunch. Anyone interested should call Mom or Dad before 3:00 P.M. on Thursday. You will be paid when the job is completed. *Taxes will be taken out of your check.*

If you handle this situation as if it were a real business opportunity, your kids will get serious, too. If you're lax, they'll model your behavior. If you expect them to come with a good attitude, have one yourself. If you expect them to be on time, don't you show up thirty minutes late. Our kids follow our lead.

EMPLOYER ALERT

Let your kids know that it's not enough for *them* to be satisfied with the job they've done. It must pass supervisor satisfaction tests. Letting them know this will prepare them for real on-the-job experiences. It is therefore necessary for them to know the performance expectations before they begin work. Also let them know that if they walk out in the middle of a job, they won't be paid.

Let's say your ten-year-old daughter tells you she's interested in making some extra money, but she shows up for work an hour late without so much as a courtesy call beforehand. What do you do? What if she says she was sick as a dog? Do you let her slide? Absolutely not. In fact, you have a few options: send her back home, dock her pay, or blow it off. I don't recommend blowing it off; that would be disastrous. But give this some serious thought. I hate it when people show up late, especially when they don't call to say they're going to be late. Things come up, yes, but we have to let our kids know that while Mom or Dad may be an understanding boss, not everyone else is. This is also an opportunity to teach several important life skills, such as responsibility, accountability, and consequences for actions.

Teaching Your Kids About Honesty

This is a biggie. The only time we tend to talk about honesty is when our kids have been dishonest. But before your kids give you an eye-opening experience, find out where they fall on the honesty scale. Here are a few tests to use:

- Simply ask what they would do if someone gave them too much change at the store.
- Leave a $5 bill on the kitchen table and see what happens.
- Send your kid to the store and see if she hands you the change without your asking for it.

These tests are not designed to set your kids up or trick them. But, face it, we are not with our kids twenty-four hours a day and cannot know what's going on with them 100 percent of the time. It's better that we find out firsthand if our kids are going astray. Plus, sometimes kids need us to make those gray areas about honesty clearer for them. They may think that Mommy's money is their money. They may think that the man at the grocery store ought to be more careful and pay more attention to his math skills.

By talking to your child after something disappears from your wallet, you're giving your child a chance to tell you what she was thinking, and you're also teaching a valuable lesson that won't result in a trip to the county jail or a detention home.

A point in case: I asked my daughter, who had just turned seven, to write an essay entitled "What Would I Do If I Found a $50 Bill Lying on the Sidewalk?" This essay was truly eye-opening. First of all, she was excited about writing this essay, and I couldn't understand why . . . until I got her finished essay.

She started off by saying that $50 was a lot of money, and then she named all the ways she would enjoy "her" new $50. I was astounded. The prospect of having a fresh new $50 bill would excite almost any kid. Anyway, I finished reading the essay, and then we had a discussion. I asked her whose money the $50 was, to which she responded that it was hers because she'd found it. She went on to laugh and say, "Finders keepers, losers weepers." And although her spending spree included a special gift for me, I wasn't thrilled that this child hadn't even entertained the thought that the money was not hers. I asked her if she thought the $50 had just fallen from the sky or if it could've possibly belonged to someone else. "Oh! I guess someone could've lost it, huh, Mommy?" Phewww! There was hope, I thought. By the end of the conversation I had navigated her to at least consider looking for the owner if she ever found anything, not just money.

Now do you see why it's important to talk to your kids? I'd never found anything while she was with me, so she had no idea what I would do in such a situation. Fortunately, a few weeks later we were at the mall. I made a phone call at the pay phone. When I hung up, change poured out of the phone. She got so excited as she collected the quarters, nickels, and dimes.

"Look, Mom!" I looked at her but didn't say a word. She smiled. "It's not ours, so we'll just leave it here, right?"

"Right," I answered. "I will call the people who own that particular phone and tell them that their phone is giving money away. How 'bout that?"

She laughed and we went home. Brittany now knows that I walk the talk. This is very important for our kids. We have to stop telling them to do as we say and not as we do. Remember, young kids don't have a clear idea of time. *Soon* to them is tomorrow. So take a tip: Say what you mean or don't say it at all.

What Stealing Is All About

I have read that almost all kids experiment on some level with stealing or shoplifting. But how far will they go to have what they want? I've wondered if the act of stealing is about possessing something or about power. I don't know. I spoke with a young man who had been to prison for theft. When I asked him why he stole things, he said it was because he didn't think anyone was smart enough to catch him or strong enough to say something to him. Hmmm . . . I thought about this for a long time.

Essentially this brother was flirting with the system and daring it to discipline him. He wanted to be taught a lesson. He was not destitute; he was the son of a well-known attorney. The first thing he ever stole was a soft drink. He says the clerk saw him take it but didn't say a word. He realized that someone was scared of him because he was a young black male. "Of *me?*" he said. So he continued to take things because he kept getting the same reaction from nearly every adult or authority figure he encountered. I sat across from this clean-shaven, handsome black man and marveled. He did not intend to continue stealing. It became a game to him. Finally, he says he realized that he was a criminal, and once he had adopted a "criminal mentality," he had a difficult time turning his life around. He was gone, as he said.

WHAT DO I DO IF MY CHILD STEALS SOMETHING?

The first thing you need to do is have a talk with your child. I know parents who have skipped the conversation and spanked the child instead, never exploring the "whys" of his behavior. Big mistake. Sometimes kids are simply acting out, wanting some attention. And in many cases, negative attention is better than no attention at all. It's very important for your child to understand that stealing, taking something that is not hers, is wrong and punishable by law. I would recommend that the child (not you) return whatever was stolen, apologize to the owner, and then do community service work. Your child may also benefit from some form of counseling or psychotherapy.

Losing Stuff

Q. If your five-year-old received $10 from her grandmother and left it lying in the middle of the bathroom floor, what should you do?

A. Swoop in and put it in the family bank. Your child has to understand that money is valuable and shouldn't be left lying around.

When a child loses something, you basically have three choices: Make 'em pay for it, make 'em sweat bullets, or make 'em wait it out. The right choice is the one that conveys to your child that carelessness is a serious offense, the one that clearly states that you will not be covering for them.

Making 'em pay for it: This can be done by deducting from allowances or bonuses.

Making 'em sweat it out: This is a minor torture device designed to let them think about what they've done.

Making 'em wait it out: This requires a strong stomach because they will be complaining from the day they got into trouble until the day they can replace the item (for example, if they lose a portable CD player and you tell them that they must wait a year to buy another one).

Q. My ten-year-old came home crying today because she lost a library book. It costs $15.95, but he gets only $5 a week allowance. Should I pay it for him?

A. Are you crazy? Start paying his bills, and you'll be paying them when he's collecting Social Security. Instead, use this incident to teach accountability and responsibility. By now you've already explained that personal expenses such as penalties and things that are lost are replaced by taking the money out of their allowance.

Allowances Explained

Why give an allowance? Because it teaches valuable lessons, including ones about sharing in family resources. Historically we haven't given our kids allowances, not necessarily because we didn't see the value but because we didn't necessarily have it to spare—or so we thought.

Allowances are a great way to introduce your kids to money. They teach responsibility, budgeting, and money management, among other things. Kids need a sense of their own money. Having money feels good, and our kids need to know how that feels. A lot of poor kids steal not because they're deviants but because they don't know what it feels like to have something that's all theirs. And this feeling is even better when they've earned the money. This is one reason drug dealers target inner-city kids for employment: Destitution and desperation make good prospects when fast money is involved. A kid who has never held a $5 bill in his hand salivates at the thought of having a wad of fifties in his pocket.

I know how it feels to be on a tight budget, but an allowance needs to be figured into the budget. Even if it's only a few dollars a month, you will be doing your child a big favor.

> Q. *Should kids work for their allowance?*
>
> A. Experts say it depends on your goals as parents.
>   If your goal is to teach that nothing in this life
>   is free, then, yes, they should. If your goal is to
>   teach kids to manage money, then the answer
>   is no. In both cases I recommend that basic
>   chores be unpaid and that you offer special jobs
>   for pay.

DETERMINING HOW MUCH TO GIVE

First of all, *you* don't make this decision—not entirely.
The best thing to do is sit down with your child, with a
sheet of paper and a pen in hand. Then the two of you
can make a list of her *monthly* needs and expenses.
Break it down on paper by the week for young kids.
Another idea is to give your child a monthly allowance
of one dollar per year of life. A seven-year-old receives
$7, a ten-year-old receives $10, and so on.

If you go the straight expenses route, you should
include such things as lunch and recreation money.
Once you come up with a monthly total, determine
how much should be spent weekly. You want the allowance to be big enough so that there's something to
manage, but not so big that you'll go into cardiac arrest
if your child squanders it before the month is over.

The big question is whether you should dole it out
all at once or biweekly or weekly. It all depends on you.
I give my eight-year-old money for the week on Sunday.
She then has to decide if she wants to have milk and
popcorn one day, which means there would be one day
that she would not have milk money or she would not

have money for a matinee on Saturday. She takes enough food in her lunch box, as far as I'm concerned, but if she wants to use part of her weekly allowance on a snack of her choice, I don't object. I explain to her when I hand over the cash, "This is *it*. No more." And her response is always the same: "Yes, ma'am, I know." She's been on the program for nearly a year and has never lost her lunch money, and she has never had to ask me for more money before the week's over. And she's only seven. It all depends on how firm you're willing to be with your kids. If you give your child $20 for the month and by day five she has only $5 remaining, that's not *your* problem. No matter how much they beg, sob, or weep, sometimes they have to learn the hard way. It's our job to make sure they know that money is not an easy-come-easy-go commodity.

Docking Allowances and Other Penalties

Let's say you told your daughter to take out the trash, and she forgot to do it. You tell her again, and she forgets again. The third time you call her to you and tell her that her allowance for the week has been docked because you had to tell her three times to do a task. She will scoff and howl, but I bet she'll get off her tush a lot sooner the next time!

But maybe she won't . . . ahhhh. What if you have a child who doesn't care about money? That means she couldn't care less that you docked her allowance. What then? Well, I say hit 'em where it hurts. That's why you have to know your kids. What is important to your daughter? Privileges, freedom, playing video games, what? Find out. And once you find out, make sure she knows that failure to fulfill her responsibilities at home or at school may result in consequences that matter to her.

Allowance and *Schoolwork* have nothing to do with each other, so it is not a topic of discussion. There are parents who pay their kids to learn. If you're doing this, shame on you! Education is its own reward. Let's not confuse our kids. If your children bring home excellent marks, give 'em a hug, a kiss, a certificate, a pat on the back, a high five—not a green five.

ALLOWANCE TIPS

- Give at the beginning of the month to encourage saving and budgeting.
- Make it large enough so that a portion *can* be saved.
- Decide on raise periods and publish these.
- Don't decrease allowances for inappropriate behavior.
- Make your children accountable for their allowance.

Advances, Raises, Bonuses, and Rewards

Let's say your son wants to go to Venice Beach for spring break, and the trip, including lodging, will run close to $300. He has a trip jar because he likes to travel, but he has only $195 in it. Should you advance him the $105?

There are several things to consider. Can you afford to advance that kind of money? How long has he known about this trip? Has he blown his money, or has he been diligent in saving? Is there enough time for him to work for this money? Has he been responsible to date? I know how much we sometimes want our children to have a good time, and we feel bad when we don't have the money. But the last thing you want to do is go into debt over a spring break trip. If you've done your job well, your son has already thought of a few options on his own.

Another event that may occur is your child coming to you and asking for a raise. That is not a bad thing. I recommend having a discussion about raises when you institute your allowance system. Explain that raises will not be granted arbitrarily or just because a child is finding new ways to blow his current allowance. But if your child can justify the need for an increase in allowance, you certainly should be open to the idea.

Besides, this process prepares kids for the working world, where people in general are continually frustrated with infrequent pay raises. In many cases it's not that people don't deserve raises, it's that people are intimidated by the whole raise process and don't know how to ask for one. By encouraging your children to present their cases in a persuasive manner, you are teaching them not only good communication but also solid negotiation skills. You also introduce them to compromise and rejection. It may be that you won't go the distance with their request, but you might meet them halfway.

Bonuses are another matter; they are usually associated with working and can be tricky. When should kids be given bonuses? Even Sergeant Harris gives an occasional bonus. A bonus doesn't have to be money, though. A bonus or a reward can and should come in many forms. We don't want our kids to always ask us how much money they are going to get for helping out, do we? One day I asked my daughter to do something, and she looked at me and quipped, "Are you gonna pay me?" She wasn't belligerent; she really wanted to be clear on whether the job was a paid or unpaid task. I laughed quietly to myself, and told her it was unpaid.

Be sure to reward for work that is above and beyond the call of duty and responsibility. If your child does an extra good job of cleaning the gutter, take him to that movie he's been dying to see but didn't have the money for.

There are also non-monetary rewards. If you have a computer, you can create a certificate, especially if you have a nifty graphics software program. When Brittany does something outstanding, I make a certificate for her, and the look on her face is worth a million dollars. She hangs all her certificates on her wall so she gets constant reinforcement that she has done a great job.

I encourage Brittany to put her recognition in view. When she learned to swim last summer, I gave her an old gold medal of mine. It hangs on her door, and it's one of her prized possessions. She's seven, but certificates work for just about anybody. Don't underestimate a homemade certificate. The key is to vary the reward, especially when it's not monetary.

HONOR AND RECOGNIZE

At home I recently instituted something I've done most of my professional life—a Dr. Feelgood Board. That's right—for less than $10 you can make your home a place where positive energy and empowerment reside. Simply get a cork-type board that uses pushpins so you can tack up notices of praise and recognition. Each family member must put up something he or she feels good about that happened or that he or she did that week. Each person can submit more than one, but one is the minimum. This is an awesome way to keep your house a home.

Raising Smart Shoppers

Most children begin their first financial lessons at the grocery store, so you need to make the most of those trips to the supermarket. Don't just plop little Joni in that seat and take off down the aisle, particularly if she is at counting age. Here's a good time to talk to yourself. Kids are listening to you anyway, so you may as well let the dialogue be part of the lesson. Say things like "Hmm, let's see. This cereal is $2.99 and this one is $3.99, but I'm getting more for my money." Joni's shopping experience therefore becomes more than just throwing things in the steel basket with wheels.

The next time you're grocery-shopping with your young kids, take them to the cereal aisle and hand them $4. Tell them to get two boxes of cereal that the family likes. See what happens.

When we shop department stores and pay department-store prices, we're telling our kids to do the same. When we don't look for sales and bargains, we're telling our kids to do the same. When we buy brand-name everything, we're telling our kids to do the same. Yet we get angry when our kids want the priciest jeans on the rack. We say things like "Does this girl think money grows on trees?" Of course she does—she sees Dad and Mom shop like there's no tomorrow and as if there were a money tree in the backyard.

BUYING FADS AND TRENDS

I remember when I was a seventh grader, everybody was wearing Earth shoes. Remember Earth shoes? Well, I wanted this pair with a wavy rubber sole. When my mom and I went shopping, they didn't have them at the time, so my mom made me get a disgusting brown pair with a thick, ugly, eraser-looking heel. I was incensed. I said I hated them. What did she do? She paid for them, and off we went.

My mother's reason for getting those shoes was "quality before fashion," two terms that I later learned didn't have to be mutually exclusive. Mom said those were "good shoes," another phrase I came to hate, and she wasn't buying me any cheap shoes just to go to the store the next month to buy a new pair. I didn't value this lesson until much later—after I'd spent money on little faddish items that lasted only a week. We have to teach our kids about fads, trends, and the latest rages. Teach them to value long-term enjoyment, not what's hot for the moment.

It's hard to teach a kid to exercise discipline, to say that this, too, shall pass when everywhere you turn there's some kind of hype trying to get your money. So ask your child, "Are you just buying this because the kid on the television says it's cool to have, or do you really want it? I heard you talking about that interactive computer game a few weeks ago. . . ." You get the idea. Help them see how they are being bombarded with "buy me" messages, which may be the reason they want a particular item.

A good idea is to have a cool-down period of a week or two. For example, if your child wants an item that you think is motivated by the "me, too, syndrome," tell him the item is under consideration for the allotted cool-down period. If he's still on fire for it after that period, then he can present it to you again. Sometimes the enthusiasm for an item dies, especially if it truly was the result of slick advertising or momentary peer pressure. So hang in there—don't give in immediately.

SHOPPING TIPS

- Shop outlet malls.
- Shop around for best deals.
- Clip and use coupons.
- Pick up the supermarket circulars.
- Scout out the competition for better prices.
- Buy things when they're on *sale*.
- Ask service personnel questions about the products you buy.
- Compare brand-name products with store or generic brands.
- Shop a season ahead or for end-of-season bargains.
- Know the store's return and exchange policies.
- Keep receipts.
- Routinely ask to see the manager.

We have to begin early to teach our kids about shopping because their buying preferences are formed early. Kids who are nine, ten, or eleven years old are well into making their choices about clothes, music, and so on. So this is the prime time to get into what I call the "really reallies" of their choices. And keep in mind that the lesson you teach your twelve-year-old might not be the same as the one for your fifteen-year-old. The principle may be the same, but the lesson plan would probably be different.

Learning the Value of Money

Kids, unless they're savvy money managers, don't have an appreciation for the value of money. They don't know how to stretch a dollar. Use this game to illustrate a powerful money lesson. Ask your kids to write what different money amounts can buy, while you do the same. For example: $20 buys ———; $50 buys ———; $5 buys ———. Let them look around the house. Then compare your lists. On your kids' lists will probably be tons of perishable items—clothing and perhaps games. On your list will be grocery items, utilities, and so forth. These are things they probably will not have thought about, and that's okay. You don't want to scold them because their lists didn't match yours. You want them to have a greater appreciation for the value of the green, period. The nice thing about this particular exercise is that your kids will be more empathetic when you say such things as "That's our meal money for the week" or "I have just enough gas money to last until the end of the month."

Saving Money

"What is a bank?" I asked a friend's five-year-old this question, and he answered, "A place where I get a sucker every time I go there. The lady at the desk gives Mommy money and me candy." Brittany wants to know where they keep everyone's money, and will they (the bank personnel) steal it.

Explaining the banking system to a six-year-old is interesting. One way to explain it is by talking to them about things they have firsthand knowledge of—their piggy banks. Here's an example.

> "Lisa, I noticed that you put your $2 in your bank in your room. Why?"
>
> "Because it's safe there."
>
> "And what if you wanted to buy something?"
>
> "Then I would go to my bank, open it up, and take out the money I needed. Then I'd shut it and put it back in my drawer."
>
> "What if I wanted to borrow some of your money? What would you do?"
>
> "I'd ask you how much you needed, and then I'd go and get it out."

DEVELOPING SAVINGS SKILLS

There are many ways to increase the amount you are able to save. Most people think the most effective way to save is simply to take it off the top of your income on a regular basis. That's not wrong—in fact, it's good—but another way is to reduce your expenses systematically. Let's say you have a credit card balance of $500, and you're paying monthly finance charges. By paying off this debt, you'll be able to put that finance charge into savings. *Voilà!* You've just increased your savings by reducing your expenses. Teach your kids this lesson. If they're always complaining about being a dollar short, sit them down and talk about eliminating unnecessary expenses, such as snacks, videos, games, and so forth.

With kids, anything you introduce them to in a fun, energetic manner is likely to be well received. The "By gosh, you are going to save money if it's the last thing you do" approach won't have the same effect as "Hey, you know that $10 you got for your birthday? How about letting me show you how to make it $20. Wouldn't that be great?" Heck, I'm excited, and it's not even my $20!

This is a great time to talk to your kids about interest. Yes, kids as young as eight can grasp the basic concepts of interest, so don't underestimate them.

MATCHING SAVINGS

If you really want to excite your kids about saving, offer to match their savings on an annual basis. Be careful, though: You need to be saving throughout the year so you can be sure that you don't write a bouncing check on payday. Think of how disappointed your child would be—after working really hard at saving and getting fired up at the prospect of seeing his cash doubled—to see you stutter and stammer around on judgment day. If you don't believe you can match your child's savings dollar for dollar, offer something you can do, such as ten cents on the dollar or fifty cents on the dollar. Whatever amount you decide, it'll be more than the child had, and she'll get excited and motivated as well.

Credit Cards

My daughter has never seen me use a credit card. Wow! I wonder what she thinks about credit cards. She has asked me about them and knows that I have one, but she has never seen me pay for something with it. One day recently she asked me why I never buy anything with my credit card. I told her that I didn't want to owe anyone anything and that if I want something and don't have the cash for it, I wait until I do.

Yes, you need to discuss credit cards with your seven-year-olds and early adolescents. They can understand. Remember, advertising is everywhere. If you've used your credit card, surely your children are curious as to how you were able to walk up to the counter, get a total from the store clerk, whip out a flat, eye-catching plastic card, and walk away with your purchase. And even if they haven't asked you about that little magical card, they've wondered. So take the curiosity out of the game and initiate a conversation about the card.

First, take out one of your credit cards (you know you have one) and let your child look at it, examine it. Ask her to tell you how she thinks it works. Listen carefully and then begin the "real" explanation. Credit cards are borrowed money—money you borrow from a bank, a department store, or some other institution. When you borrow this money, you are charged interest. The interest varies depending on how much the lender wants to charge. As a borrower you are given a "grace period" to repay the money, typically thirty days. If you repay the entire amount you borrowed (that is, charged), you are not assessed interest. If you do not pay "the amount in full," you must pay the amount you borrowed plus interest.

When explaining this to your child, it would be helpful if you gave a real-life example and involved your child. The practice will be invaluable.

CREDIT, ANYONE?

For grins and to teach a lesson, pick up a credit card application and sit down with your son or daughter to complete it. Don't get one of those short forms; they don't ask you for enough information to teach the lessons your kids need to know. Get a long version, the one that gets all up in your business. Take the form and complete it, line by line, in the presence of your preteen. Discuss each section you complete. Here are some sample questions and comments.

1. Why do you think they want to know how much money I make? This may be obvious to you and me but not to an eleven-year-old.
Lesson: Teach how creditors determine how much credit to give you.

2. Do you know what gross income is?
Lesson: Teach net versus gross income and the importance of each.

3. Why do you think they want to know if I own or rent a house?
Lesson: Teach about perception of owning versus renting, net worth, collateral, and so forth, depending on the age and maturity of your child.

4. Why do they want the names of three references?
Lesson: Teach the importance of good credit ratings and who will say what about you.

5. Why do you think they want my bank account information?

Lesson: Once the credit card company has your information, it knows the amounts of money that flow through your account, who is being paid, how much, and so forth.

These are just a few sample questions for you to use. You can develop others.

Checks

Just as you explained how credit cards work, you also need to explain personal checks. Once they understand the banking system, children generally understand that when you write a check, it's just like cash. They also know that no one can write checks on your account except those you designate, just as no one can go into little Joni's bank except her. The best way to drive this skill home is to set up a bank in your home, make up checks, and allow them to establish an account. We'll discuss this in more detail later.

Conflict in the Hood

The preteen stage is where real conflict begins to surface. Preteens are starting to express their opinions, make choices, disagree, and so forth. More power to them. But just how do we as parents effectively handle such conflict? Sometimes we have to lay down the law. But you'll find there are many other alternatives that enable you to remain the authority figure in your home while at the same time allowing you to teach your child a very important money management skill.

Let's take a real example. Brittany once insisted that she was going to wear a pair of lightweight stretch pants to school on the following Monday. It was Saturday, and the forecast said that thirty degrees would be the high for Monday. I told her this, and she said, "Well, maybe by Monday it'll change, it'll be warmer." Monday came, and it was not thirty, it was nineteen when she woke up. She put on the pants, and when I came out of my room, she announced that she was ready to go. I told her to change to a warmer pair of pants. She pitched a mild protest but changed just the same.

Brittany was expressing her desires and preferences, and that was good. I'd hate to have to tell her to make her every move. By the same token, as parents we have to be ready to exercise our better judgment, which is the result of years of experience and making mistakes, right?

The same is true where money is concerned. Let's say you give your son an allowance of $5 a month. He wants to buy a pair of Nike socks. You think $5 is an insane amount of money for a pair of socks, and you tell him so. He says it's his money, and this gives him the right to do as he pleases even if you disagree. What do you do? Well, before we jump to either side, let's ask a few questions.

Is there a house rule which says that certain percentages must go to savings? If so, does he have enough in his spending bank to buy the socks? If so, then your son is right. The rules espoused in this book say that the Now or Spending funds can be spent on anything the child desires *unless* the purchase directly conflicts with family values.

Yeah, Fran, but isn't this placing restrictions on

their spending? Yes, it is. That's one of the things that separates great parents from good ones. The spending money should not have monster restrictions put on it, but some restrictions are needed. For example, if profanity and pornography are not consistent with the values you are teaching your kids, then music containing vulgarity and films of a pornographic nature cannot be tolerated under any circumstances.

Trading, Lending, and Borrowing

These are the prime ages for all three of these behaviors. Children are starting to notice and to want what they don't have. In the event that you won't purchase what your child wants, he may seek to have it anyway—and this includes money.

Trading, the act of exchanging goods, is quite common among kids. There's nothing inherently wrong with trading—until there's an imbalance of exchange. In other words, you don't want your kids taking advantage of other kids, and you don't want your kids getting the short end of the stick, either. In trading, kids should strive for equity. Penny-for-penny cost can't always be guaranteed, but the transaction should at least be in the same ballpark.

What if your child trades an autographed picture of Nelson Mandela for a Kris Kross compact disc? Was this an even exchange? At first glance it doesn't appear to be. But what if your daughter didn't really know the value (and I'm not talking about retail here) of her photo? What if she didn't mind parting with it? What do you do? My advice is to talk to her about the different types of value and then encourage her to discuss any trading opportunities with you before she does anything. What you don't want to do is scold her for making a decision that you would not have made. Instead, ask her to share with you the factors that were involved in her decision-making process.

Lending is a serious step toward independence. After all, it is your kids' money, toys, clothes, and so forth. They may feel perfectly comfortable letting a friend or family member borrow them.

On Tuesday an eight-year-old schoolmate, Billy, asks your son for thirty cents for a carton of milk. Your son gives it to him and asks no questions. The next three days the same thing happens. On Friday your son says that Billy owes him $1.20, and he wants his money. Do you march up to the school and demand to see little Billy? Do you call Billy's parents and demand the money? Do you blow it off and tell your son not to keep giving Billy his money? Do you have a serious talk with your son about smart lending?

Believe it or not, all these options have at one time been chosen by a parent who believed he was doing the right thing. The most appropriate choice is the one that helps your child walk away from the experience with some dignity and a lesson learned. In this case, prevention is the key. That is why it is so important to discuss the concepts of *In the Black* with your kids on a regular, systematic basis.

How do you make smart lenders out of your kids? First, you let them know they have the right to say no— to whomever. That's the main thing. Feeling confident enough to say no is empowering, and we want our kids to understand that no one has the right to take anything from them. But when peers ask to borrow something, sometimes our kids are uncomfortable handling this situation. They may fear rejection or the loss of status or friendship.

I discourage borrowing between young friends, period, but let's say one of your children approaches another for a small loan, maybe $3. Is this okay? Sure, but the questions that should routinely be asked apply to family members as well: How much do you want? What do you need it for? When are you going to repay it?

This process is not only healthy, it gets our kids ready for the real world. When you apply for a bank loan, they ask you: How much do you want? What do you need it for? And when are you going to repay it? Why should the rules be any different for little borrowers? They shouldn't.

A final note: In teaching your kids about borrowing and lending, it is important to tell them that neither should be viewed as shameful or bad. Borrowing is sometimes necessary. Teach your kids to strive to achieve a win-win situation—one that both the lender and the borrower can live with.

SAMPLE SKILLS AND KNOWLEDGE
FOR YOUR PRETEENS

At minimum, your preteens should know the following:

To make change: Be able to go to the store and figure out how much money to give and to get back.

Money equivalents: Know, for example, that two $50 bills equal one $100 bill.

How much it costs to run a household: Know that $5 won't pay the mortgage.

Budgeting: Know how to manage money so that all obligations are met.

Measurements: What a cup of sugar looks like. What an eight-ounce glass of water is.

Shoplifting or stealing isn't a game: Know the difference between what is theirs and what is not.

Banking system: Know how banks work and what interest is. Know how checks and credit cards work.

Credit: Know that credit card purchases are more expensive than cash purchases.

THE TERRIFIC . . . UH, TRYING TEENS

We need what money cannot buy and what affluence is too beggarly to purchase. . . . I am not aiming to enlist a fanatical crusade against the desire for riches but I do protest against chaining down the soul, with its Heaven endowed facilities and God-given attributes, to the one idea of getting money as stepping into power or even gaining our rights in common with others. The respect that is only bought by gold is not worth much.

—FRANCES HARPER

Frequently Asked Questions About Teenagers

Here are some of the most common questions that parents have concerning money and teens:

Q. *My fifteen-year-old has really gotten into music. Every time I turn around he's buying Ice Cube, Ginuwine, or some other food- or drink-article–named singer's latest CD. I fear that he's using his lunch money to buy music. What should we do?*

A. Obviously this is about whether your child is eating properly or not and that's a common problem among teens who perceive that they're just fine and that a bag of chips is lunch sometimes. As parents we have to monitor their purchases when it threatens their health and well-being. I'd advise that you sit your son down and help him develop a plan for meeting his nutritional needs as well as his desire to buy music. Perhaps your son will ask you to buy certain things so that he can take a sack lunch for two weeks to cover the cost of his music. Be firm and tell him that not eating or not eating properly could pose a serious health issue.

Q. *My thirteen-year-old will not spend his money. He gets $40 a week for an allowance, and he keeps it all in a safe place in his bedroom. Is this normal?*

A. Normal is a matter of opinion, but your son's behavior definitely warrants your attention. It's important to approach him by saying that you're curious. Avoid asking, at least at the outset, "Why are you hoarding all your money in a jar under your bed?" That sounds a bit judgmental even if you don't actually feel that you're judging him. He may immediately become defensive. Try this approach: "Son, I notice you're saving a lot of your money. That's great. Is there something special you've got your eyes on buying or doing?" Your goal is to get to the heart of *why* he's so concerned about holding on to every single penny he gets. And it may be that he has seen this pattern in the household. Or it may be the direct opposite—he's gotten a message that there's never enough money; he may be safeguarding against a similar situation and wants to be sure that he always has money.

Q. *My daughter is about to graduate from high school, as is her boyfriend. She has saved nearly $500 from her employment and is dead set on buying this young man an expensive watch. What can I do, if anything, to stop her from doing this?*

A. This is a tough one for several reasons. First, your daughter is a young adult who has to learn that there are consequences for her behavior, if she hasn't learned this already. In other words, whether *you* would make this buying decision isn't the issue here. Second, $500 is a lot to spend on *anyone*, yet for some reason your daughter is ready to make such an investment. Again, dialogue is essential. Ask her why she has chosen this particular gift. And it is okay to tell her that you feel it is a bit elaborate. Could it be that your daughter feels splurging on a big, showy gift reveals her love or commitment to this young man? If this is the case, then she certainly needs to have a discussion with you (or a professional) about esteem and self-worth. Your daughter may be a bit mixed up.

Q. *My fifteen-year-old son just came home and announced that he needs $115 for a debt he owes to a* *neighbor. I didn't even know he had borrowed any money, and now he wants us to pay this child. We are good friends with the parents and don't want to ruin our relationship. What should we do?*

A. Well, I'll tell you what you shouldn't do . . . pay your son's debt! Since you have a good relationship with the child's parents, I'd recommend telling your son that you will be talking about it with his friend's parents and that a discussion with him will follow. You may leave the parents' meeting with some valuable information, such as details of the debt that you may not have gotten from your son. Once you're ready to talk to your son, explain, first, that you will not be repaying the debt—that he owes it. Allow him the time to explain how the debt was incurred. Then tell him that you expect him to figure out a way to repay the debt within a reasonable period of time (say, three months).

Q. *My fourteen-year-old daughter has a newfound interest in makeup and is always experimenting with my cosmetics. I usually don't mind, but occasionally she leaves the containers open or lipstick gets on my other items. What should I do?*

A. First, talk to your daughter about her newfound interest. It's always a good idea to inquire when new behaviors or interests pop up in our children's lives. Your daughter could just be going through the usual self-exploratory stages of adolescence, or she could be succumbing to peer pressure. In either case, you shouldn't foot the bill. Discuss with your daughter, first, the importance of asking permission to use something that doesn't belong to her and the responsibility associated with usage once permission is granted. Then suggest that she spend her allowance on her own cosmetics. In fact, a trip to the local cosmetics counter might be a great mother-daughter outing.

A Word or Two About Teens

Whoever named the twos "terrible" obviously didn't have a teenager in the house at that time. Because the teen years are often times of self-discovery and independence, they are frequently the most turbulent years for both parents and teens. *We* know nothing, and they know *everything*. They tend to have their minds made up about their preferences, but these choices may still be influenced by peers and advertisements. So be the filter and continue to talk to them about the "whys" of their choices on all fronts, but particularly money.

Get into the nuts and bolts of markup, packaging, and image. Did you know that a $20 tube of lipstick could cost less than four cents to make? Four cents! Yet consumer ignorance especially among blacks is ridiculously high. Talk to them about those Hilfiger undershorts and those Nike headbands that we buy for the symbol they represent. Believe me, when I'm gone, nobody will be saying, "You know the wonderful thing about Fran was that she drove a twin-cylinder, 800-horsepower vehicle with a 50-CD changer, and she wore the cutest clothes," and so forth. Ultimately, what we are remembered for—and what I'd much rather be revered for—is what we gave, not what we had. This is a valuable lesson to teach not only our teens but also ourselves.

SOME COMMON QUESTIONS TEENAGERS ASK

Why pay the full $150 on your credit card bill when you can pay only $20?

If I still have checks, do I still have money in the bank?

What if I see something that I want that costs $12.99 and I have only $12.50, can I write a check and will the bank spot me the forty-nine cents?

What's wrong with using my credit card when I also have cash?

Listen up! What your kids *don't* know about money *can* and *will* hurt them. Developing bad financial habits—as kids can and frequently do—leads to greater problems as they head into adulthood.

If you're wondering what you can do to help your teenagers, let me tell you that the answer is "A lot. Much. Tons." Precisely because they think they know everything and are pretty set in their ways, they have much to learn about money management—especially if you're just now starting to teach them. With teenagers you'll find the lessons aren't all that different, it's the approach that's different.

What you have to do is decide where your teenager is today. The principles of earlier sections can be applied to your teens. In fact, I recommend that you take your teen through all the sections of the book in order to get a really clear picture of where she is and the work you have ahead of you.

Your first task is to remember that as much as you

may hate to admit it, you were once a teenager. Yes, you—the person who makes all the right decisions and never goofs up—were a teenager. If you can hold on to that thought, you are in good shape. You will need to remember it when your impatient teenager stares at you as you attempt to teach her something. You will need to remember it when he shrugs and says something like "Yeah, yeah, I got it, Dad." You will need to remember it when your teenager forgets what you just told her. So don't forget. In fact, say it loud right now: I WAS ONCE A TEENAGER. Again: I WAS ONCE A TEENAGER. Good.

Communicating with Teenagers

Now on to the real teenagers of the house. The key is communication, solid and open communication. If you have already established open lines of communication with your children, great. Today's teenagers want the same things we wanted: to be trusted, viewed as responsible young adults, and respected for their individuality. Weren't those a few of the things we wished and prayed our parents would get through their heads?

It's equally important to acknowledge that as parents we have some of the same fears our parents had about our transition from kidsville to adulthood, and we want our kids to be safe, smart decision-makers. There are no hard-and-fast rules for making this work in your household. Unfortunately, life holds no guarantees, but I will tell you this: If developing money skills is important to you, your kids will hear and see this, and like everything else, they will give you at least an occasional portion of their attention.

Remember, just as young kids mature at different rates, so do teenagers. You may be able to go fast with some teenagers but need to proceed slower with others. If you have an enthusiastic and eager child, go for it. By the same token, don't get too impatient with kids who appear apathetic or uninterested at first. Keep making it meaningful and fun, and they'll come around.

HOW TO TALK TO TEENS

Today's lingo is no stranger than ours was to our parents, so don't even go there. Somehow, other generations preferred the word "chicks" to "hos" when talking about women, but if you ask me, I'm neither—so why not call me what I am? A woman. But when talking to your kids, you may have to dabble in their language occasionally. I am not advocating that you pretend your kids don't have a handle on the English language, I'm just suggesting that you make this job a little interesting. Don't be stiff. It's possible to convey a serious message using ordinary language. Teenagers want to feel that you respect their intelligence and ability to grasp difficult concepts. So avoid saying things like "This may be a little over your head" or "George's daughter, Selina, has been doing this for two years."

Speak their language. Your kids will appreciate the effort. They may laugh, but at least you'll have their attention. You should have seen the look on my twenty-one-year-old brother's face when I said something like "Oh, so you flexin' for yo boys, huh?" No matter how many times or how long I talk "cool," the response is always the same: laughter. He was impressed, he admits, that I know these words, that I'm not stuck in the Stone Age even though I'm ten years his senior.

I'm told that I was always a few years older than my chronological age. My relatives say I have an old soul. But even as a mature teenager, I couldn't have known the reality of adulthood, and neither will your teenager. Teens live on earth for 182.5 days a year, and on planet La-La the other 182.5. They think they have a handle on the real world, but they don't. It's our job to prepare them as much as possible. That means providing them with as many real-life situations as we can muster up.

Talk to a teenager and nine times out of ten you'll get a heavy dose of self-praise and not enough self-accountability—criticism, some call it. You can call it what you want, but in general teenagers tend to think they've done better than they have and never as bad as they do. And they don't know nearly anything about the cost of living, salaries, and such.

So, once you start your money program with your teenager, you must do the "how much does a ——— [fill in with job title] make a year?" game. You'll be amazed at their perception of how much certain industries render.

JOB REALITY

A particularly industrious teenager may have some idea of the career he wants to pursue. If he doesn't know, don't sweat it—or him. Let's hope he figures it out by the time college graduation rolls around. If you can instill one principle in your teen, let it be that he should do what he loves, nurture what he loves, and be able to make a living at it.

This exercise is designed to give teenagers a dose of job reality. Have them research a few fields that might interest them as teenagers, not as adults. They need to find out the following information: industry outlook, what the starting salaries are and what the top people in the field make, and any preparatory skills that are needed.

Rules, Independence, and Understanding

It may sound funny, but as your kids get older, you need just as many rules as you had when they were young—and maybe more. Why? Because they are about to be dropped from the nest into the real world. When they were young, we could hold their hands and protect them to a certain degree. They have more choices before them as teens, as well as greater consequences. I suggest that you have a serious conversation with them about the realities of life—especially money, credit, and taxes. Also remember to discuss which rules are negotiable and which are not.

Can you say independence? This is the big word in teenagers' vocabulary. Even though the word may never come out of their mouths, it's all over their behavior. (It was in ours, and it is in theirs.) Now you have to decide what independence looks like in your household—only you know what you're willing to accept.

"If you want to do what Jen does, go live with Jen." This line was never used in my house, but I'm told that some parents have used it. Whenever I had the audacity (which was rarely) to say to my mother, "So-and-so's mother is letting her do it," I was always told, "Well, this is how *we* do things here, and since this is where you live, you will do them this way. When you turn eighteen, you may leave and do them exactly as you please."

My younger brother wanted desperately to have his ears pierced while he was in high school. Our father is definitely from the old school, so Chris didn't stand a chance. When he called to ask me what *I* thought about it, he mentioned that he had the money to pay for it. It should be clear where I'm going with this: Can we allow our teenagers to do something just because they can pay for it themselves? We don't have to, so don't get yourself into a sticky situation by saying, "I'm not paying for it" or "If you can find the money, you can have it/do it." You'd be amazed at how resourceful ordinarily apathetic people can be when they want something.

But many of the problems that parents have with teenagers don't revolve around independence so much as clarity or understanding each other. We get angry with our teens when we feel that they have deliberately disobeyed us, but sometimes it's a matter of what we've said and what they've heard. Remember, they speak a different language, and they hear a different language. So it's not enough to say, "Be home at a decent hour." To a teenager a decent hour can be when the deejay at the party goes home. To you it may be unquestionably 11:30. He gets home at midnight, and you're standing at the door tapping your foot. He's still buzzing on the last song. You wonder what planet he's on to come home at that hour. He's wondering what your deal is, it's still early.

The point is to spell out what is acceptable and what is not *and* make known what will happen if those rules are broken. As with young kids, the consequences must mean something. You can't threaten to make your daughter go to bed an hour earlier than normal if she doesn't care about hitting the sack earlier. But if you know that she truly values having access to the car, you can tell her that by coming in late she'll lose privileges for three weeks. She'll more than likely pay attention and get home on time.

Setting the Financial Ground Rules

You've probably already done this on the dating front. Now it's time to get tight on the financial front. Before you hand out any allowances, advances, or bonuses, you must schedule an orientation meeting. At this meeting you will lay down the law. You are not The Great Lawgiver, but your teenagers must adhere to certain requirements. The first being attendance at your orientation.

After the first meeting, I recommend having at least a monthly Money Sense meeting that they are required to attend or they cannot receive allowances and paychecks. Here's a suggestion for your first Money Sense meeting.

Materials needed: calculator and plenty of pencils, paper, and patience.

Setting: at a table or in a circle in the family room. Serve juice and snacks. Keep the environment relaxed and open.

Call your meeting on a Saturday afternoon before family members get too involved in yardwork, Little League, or college sports. The most important thing is to be prepared for this important event. Tell your kids you want to get their opinions/input on how the household should be run. (Don't worry; their eyes will eventually go back to their normal size.) If you have a flip chart, great; if not, ask for a volunteer to record all the suggestions and ideas that come up during the session, which shouldn't be any longer than ninety minutes from start to cleanup.

Once everyone is present (attendance is mandatory), explain that as their parent you are concerned that they be good money managers. Tell them that this will be a learning experience for you, too. And since you want to do your part, you've come up with the idea of having family money meetings. Tell them what the format of the meetings will be and that you will be talking about everything from budgets to dating to cars to vacations and education. Ask them to add to the agenda any topics to be discussed. They will feel good that they have a say in what the family does or talks about.

Every meeting should be tailored to meet your particular family's needs, but as a foundation, this first meeting should typically center around answering the question: "What is money?" The central purpose is to get some dialogue around the word "money." Be sure to record what's said. You'll have some interesting things to discuss with your partner as you plan for future meetings. In fact, this first meeting will guide subsequent agendas. Have fun and don't forget to be a *facilitator*, not Mom or Dad. Don't be surprised by what you hear. Don't judge. Try not to be overly expressive with your face or body; you want them to feel free to say whatever's on their minds. Trust me: home Money Sense meetings are an excellent way to monitor your family's money pulse. Enjoy watching your family become better and better money managers as well as communicators.

INDEPENDENCE ISSUES

This section addresses some of the independence questions that come up and revolve around money. Pay close attention, your teenager is bound to bring up one of these before it's all over.

A separate phone: I was lucky. I have older siblings, so I inherited their phone line. Sure, my mother could have had it disconnected, but she didn't—and I was eternally grateful. There were times that I blatantly disobeyed my mother and stayed on the phone past my permitted hour, but I was generally quite responsible with my phone.

If you're faced with the "When do I get my own phone?" question, you have a few response options: absolutely not, maybe, and okay. Permitting teenagers to have their own phone is one of those real-life opportunities that you can teach while they're still at home. Let's look at the advantages and disadvantages.

Advantages:

1. They won't tie up your line.
2. They'll get to go through the application process with you.
3. They'll get a firsthand look at one of the realities of adulthood.
4. They'll be empowered because it will be "their" line even if they are still living at home, but you can supervise their use.
5. They pay for it.

Disadvantages:

1. At first they will be infatuated with the new toy, which means they will have to call everybody and anybody who will listen.
2. If you're not too careful, they may run up the long-distance service. Hint: Don't allow them to hook up with a long-distance carrier. Prepaid calling cards are angels.
3. Your phone will be ringing off the hook because your teenagers are always on *their* line. Set rules. Your teenagers' friends are allowed to call only on their line.

4. They could become addicted to the phone—neglecting and forsaking all others—schoolwork, chores, and social activities. Don't let this happen. You must tell them upfront that there are guidelines for having their own phone line (time limits and hours of use). They must agree to the terms of the contract.

Alternately, a second line is a good idea

. . . if you find yourself walking in and out of the room to ask permission to use the phone.

. . . if you have two teenagers.

. . . if your spouse is constantly saying, "Every time I turn around that boy is on the phone."

Driving your car: I could drive at age thirteen, but my parents didn't know it—which means I certainly wasn't driving their car. Driving is a serious consideration, and it should not be taken lightly. It's also sort of a rite of passage, so it should not be scoffed at. Sixteen is a reasonable age to consider letting your child drive your car. But *responsible behavior* and not *age* should dictate driving privileges. Don't promise your child that she will automatically be allowed to drive on her sixteenth birthday. There's a scripture that says if God can't trust you to be faithful over a few things, how can you be trusted over many? The same principle applies to your kids. If your daughter has busted her budget consistently for the past three years, missed curfew more than she's made it, and is always a dollar short and a day late, what makes you think she's ready to get behind the wheel of your car? All these things have something to do with one another.

Some parents think that granting kids these huge responsibilities will make them become instantly responsible. Not true. In fact, you have the process transposed if you believe this. Responsible behavior *precedes* privileges and allowances.

Additionally, explain to your kids about all the responsibilities associated with driving: insurance, defensive driving, consequences of speeding, social pressures, and so forth.

Getting the kids a car: I don't really advocate flat-out buying a car for kids, even if you can afford to. The best thing to do when you see that your kids' activities are taking a toll on your schedule and vehicle is to call a team meeting. Of course, the teenagers will think an additional car is a fabulous idea. If they are in support of having a vehicle that's dedicated to them, encourage them to make a financial commitment to the venture.

Let's say you have a sixteen- and seventeen-year-old, both of whom have $3,000 in their savings accounts. A pre-owned, well-conditioned car costs at least $4,000. You may propose that they each chip in $1,000, and you and your spouse will contribute $2,000. If they immediately lose their color and go into convulsions over the thought of making such a commitment, you may have your answer. Insurance will also be necessary. As long as the kids live with you, they can be added to your insurance policy. Once they move out, they are no longer legally allowed to be carried on your policy; that's theft of services.

If you decide to buy your kids a car, be sure to take them with you. This is an excellent opportunity to expose them to a real-life situation. Let them know that they are going along for the education, that one day they will be doing this for themselves. Encourage them to take copious notes throughout the process. And make sure that you discuss what happened at the dealer when you get home.

Teenagers can't really understand the immense responsibility of having an automobile until they have more invested than emotions. Let's say they agree to contribute their money. The next challenge is developing rules for driving the car. Who gets it when? You'll need to sit down with them and set up a schedule that is posted in your home, such as this one:

Date	Driver	Departure time/place	Return By
3/12	Sean	3:30 volleyball practice	6:00 P.M.
3/12	Dru	6:30 movie/arcade	10:30 P.M.
3/13	Sean/Dru	7:45 school	4:00 P.M.
3/13	Dru	5:00 community ctr	7:30 P.M.

This log must be completed each time the car is taken. Any discrepancies must involve at least one parent. Encourage your kids to work out small details involving the use of the car. This will help them develop negotiation and communication skills.

Letting Friends Drive Their Cars

Discourage it, period.

Credit cards and ATM (or debit) cards: I read that somebody got a sixteen-year-old a credit card as a birthday gift. Were these parents insane? *Adults* have a difficult time with credit cards; it makes no sense for a sixteen-year-old, even one who is most conscientious and mature, to have a credit card. So how will our kids learn about credit cards if we don't get them one? We can teach them without their actually having hands-on experience. Conversation is an excellent tool, and so are substitute tools. You can also make a family credit card, complete with interest rates and grace periods. Issue cards to your teenagers and explain all the details for use.

Let's say I issue the Harris Card to my teenager with a $50 limit, and it carries a 12 percent APR. He would bring the card to me when he wanted money— say, $15 for a movie date. I'd explain that the $15, if paid by the due date, is free of interest. I'd send him a statement outlining the conditions for borrowing the $15.

Credit is borrowing money on someone else's terms. So if my teenager wants to borrow money from me, he has to comply with my terms or forget it. We sign an agreement, he presents his card, and I give him the $15 and a receipt for his charge. You can even have different levels of cards such as Platinum, Gold, or Silver to help them understand rewards for smart money management.

If your kids insist on having a credit card and they're old enough and employed, they can get one on their own. Encourage them to get an ATM, or debit, card instead of a credit card. Debit cards withdraw the money automatically from a checking or savings account. There's even a debit card with the Visa logo on the front. (It's no different from any other debit card except for the Visa logo.) It's cool and similar to cash because the money comes right out of the bank account. They can be used at merchants across the country, whereas other debit cards are not as widely accepted. Just make sure it's *their* debit account and not yours. Make sure they understand that each time they use the debit card, money is withdrawn from their account. And there are transaction charges, which vary.

A CREDIT CARD STORY

When my brother went to college, I ordered an extra Visa in his name for emergencies. I gave him an hour-long lecture about using the card in emergency situations only (and I was specific—volunteering to drive to the Kappa party knowing he'd have to use the card because he didn't have gas money was not an emergency), and even in those situations I expected a phone call prior to the charge if possible. He started off very well, but then I started seeing little charges on my statements. Gas for $8. Miscellaneous charges of $2 and $3. No big deal, right? It was only a couple of dollars. Wrong!

We happened to live in the same city, so I called a meeting and gave him a fair warning: *Don't abuse the privilege. This is a test and, more important, this will affect our relationship.* He apologized and offered a few lame excuses that he called reasons. I reminded him of the agreement we had and told him that the next time would be the last time. Well, a few months passed with no offenses. Then one fine day I saw a charge for pizza. I telephoned my dear brother immediately. "Cut it up" was all I said. "Cut it up. No need to send it to me— you're not a child. But do cut it up because our agreement is terminated." All I heard on the other end of the phone was air. Then a crisp "Awright." Click. And that was that. This little lesson ran me roughly $65 at the most—which he paid back in full.

If you want to give your kids a trial run at credit card responsibility, try something similar to what I did. If your risk level or tolerance for sin is not high, don't even go there. Let them learn on their own. I do think that some kind of a test run is important, although I don't necessarily think it has to be at your expense. You know your kids, and if you think they can handle it, go for it. But don't give a kid who has never shown any sign of responsibility carte blanche with your plastic.

Attention, Credit Card Users

Here are a few guidelines to instill in your kids:

- Keep all receipts until the bill comes, then go through the purchases listed on the bill.
- Do not charge if you cannot pay in full at the end of the month.
- Do not get in the habit of paying only the minimum balance.
- Do not charge perishable items, such as pizza and other snacks.
- Use for emergencies only.

Borrowing and Lending

Teenagers get into some heavy-duty borrowing and lending as they get older. Teach them to be neither a borrower nor a lender exclusively; they should find a healthy balance. The propositions become more serious. Cars, clothes, jewelry, and larger amounts of money are commonplace in high school hallways. Even though your kids may have developed strong money skills as youngsters, they can find themselves in a sticky predicament when their best buddy says, "Say, man, let me borrow your ride to run up to the store. I'll be right back." I still discourage borrowing between friends, period. In fact, as far as I'm concerned, borrowing should be a last resort.

When Brittany came home one day and pulled out an unfamiliar book, I asked her who it belonged to. "Amber," she answered. "And why do you have Amber's book?" I asked. "Well, she just let me borrow it." "And if something happens to the book while you have it, who's going to pay for it, you or Amber?" She looked at me as if I were insane. "Of course, Amber will. It's her book" was the look she gave me.

When I was growing up, my friends thought I had the strangest mother because she wouldn't let me borrow their belongings, and they couldn't borrow mine, either. At first I thought my mom was from Mars myself—until I lost my sister's sapphire pendant in the eighth grade. How in the world was I going to replace this necklace? And even if I had the money to buy another one, there was a chance that I couldn't find the exact pendant. And even if I could have found one just like hers, it still wasn't the *same* one. Do you get my point? When something is special to someone, you can't replace it even if you can. You can't duplicate the uniqueness of it, the memories attached to it, the circumstances surrounding the receiving of it. So I agree with Mom: Just *don't* do it. This is a good lesson for adults as well.

Debt

Black debt tends to increase as the income of blacks rises, according to Kelvin Boston's *Smart Money Moves for African Americans*. In other words, the more we make, the more we spend. We need to change this to the more we make, the more we save. Debt is so prevalent that there's now a television game show about it. What is debt? It's owing someone something. What can debt do? The effects of debt are far-reaching. Debt creates family tension. Debt creates emotional and psychological turmoil. Marable Manning's book *Beyond Black and White* also revealed that blacks with incomes of $5,000 actually had greater personal-debt-to-income ratios than whites with virtually no income. Additionally, for blacks with incomes below $2,500 in the early 1960s, only 25 percent had savings of $100 or more.

ALLOWANCES AND ADVANCES

Once your kids hit high school, which is generally fourteen or fifteen years old, they should be off the allowance system (or at least on part allowance, part work) and should be using money from employment for their activities. But, you may ask, what if my son is the star of the golf team, class president, or volunteers at the community center three times a week? My answer to you is that if both of you know that he has this hectic schedule during the school year, shouldn't he be saving his summer earnings in preparation for the school year? Of course he should.

I was heavily involved in school activities and really didn't have time to work during the school year, so the summers were my time to make money. You can be sympathetic to your kids' schedules, but don't let them think they're off the hook just because they have busy school year schedules. Teaching your kids to develop savings and budget plans is critical.

As your kids get older, their money needs will undoubtedly increase. Dates usually include dinner and a movie or dinner and a play—whatever. They need more money to have a good time, they explain. So let's say your seventeen-year-old has this elaborate date planned for Valentine's Day but is short about $50. She asks for an advance, and, based on her credit rating, there's no reason not to make the loan. First you must explain that this is responsible borrowing and responsible lending because her history shows that she will repay it on time.

Here are the terms of a sample advance transaction: Loanee receives $50 cash advance, interest free, on February 14, 1998. She has three weeks to repay the loan in full, which means the loan is due on March 7, 1998. Interest will commence on March 7 at the rate of 1.5 percent, and a late fee of ten cents will be added each day the loan goes unpaid.

Guidelines for advances:

- Do not remind them that they have a bill due on a particular date.
- Do not comment when you see them spending money on seemingly needless items.
- Do have a DID YOU OVERLOOK YOUR PAYMENT? invoice on their desk/dresser bright and early the day after the loan was due if they haven't paid.
- Do have a THANK YOU FOR DOING BUSINESS WITH US note on their desk/dresser bright and early the day after the loan was due if they have paid in full.
- Do praise and encourage them informally for taking care of business when they are responsible.

- Do not let them get away with telling you on the morning their loan is due that they're going to have difficulty paying it back. Encourage them to plan ahead to speak with creditors if trouble arises.
- Do stand firm. If your terms say that they cannot have another advance until the loan is paid in full, do not give another advance.
- Do consider including in the advance contract that money can be deducted systematically (not all at one time) from their allowance to cover the loan if they default. (This is a good way to introduce them to what happens when you don't pay child support or the IRS.)

Where Does Teenagers' Money Go?

How are teenagers spending their money? A 1992 survey by Teenage Research Unlimited in Northbrook, Illinois, reported that teenagers spend approximately $62 a week, which includes their money and their parents' money. And for what? Well, look at your teenagers. What do they like? Music, videos, eating out, dating activities—movies, sporting events, parties, and trips. Teens these days are also driving much more than teens did twenty years ago, so car and gas costs are part of their expenses. But just because things are different from our growing-up days, should we just sit by idly and watch them squander their money and ours? Let's break down their expenses and see how we can help them out.

Music: Encourage your kids to listen to CDs at the music store before they make the purchase. Places such as Blockbuster have stations set up for this sort of music sampling. And if there is only one song that they like, encourage them to buy the single. It usually has two or three versions of that one song, or it will give you a few free tracks.

Videos: Encourage them to seek out specials. Most video places have lower-price days, such as Two Dollar Thursday or Way Back Wednesday.

Movies: Encourage them to see matinees. This is a good suggestion not only from a budget perspective but also because of the increase in crime among teens after 7:00 P.M.

Eating out: Encourage them to find and use coupons for restaurants. Couponing is respectable no matter how sophisticated you're trying to be. And it's smart con-sumering. Encourage them to eat out at lunchtime since dinner is more expensive. And lest we forget, going dutch is perfectly acceptable, so encourage it.

Trips: Encourage them to plan ahead and discuss hotel and airline discounts, carpooling, and sharing expenses.

Gas: Encourage them to locate the lowest gas price that still provides optimal performance for their vehicle.

Sporting events: Encourage them to get involved in some way with the team that they love watching (as a towel guy/girl, keeping stats, maintenance, and so forth). Benefits for these positions often include free admission to events or substantial discounts.

Clothes budget: Encourage them to buy at least some of their own clothes (maybe you buy the big items such as coats and let them handle the rest). Again, when kids have to foot the bill, they gain a greater sense of what it really takes to live in today's world.

ADVERTISING AND TEENS

If you thought advertising consumed younger children, just watch what it's doing to our teenagers. Self-image and self-concept issues are at an all-time high for them. They're already trying to find their place in society, at school, and in the household, and here's another ad telling them they need to look better, smell sweeter, and dress like the designer of the minute. It's even more important to discuss advertising now because teens are consumers themselves. Before, they would just beg for what they wanted and pray that we got it for them. Now they are making buying decisions, and we want to make sure they are not suckers for sensationalism and slick advertisements.

PEER PRESSURE

Although this section only touches upon the effects of peer pressure, this is a critical element and should be given serious attention in your home.

During these peak teen years, everything is affecting our kids' decision-making process—hormonal changes, esteem issues, and pressures from their social contacts (which, incidentally, is not limited to their friends, but includes media messages, as well as you and your own personal relationships). When I was eight, makeup wasn't even a possibility, but when I visit my daughter's classroom, I'm amazed at the number of third-graders wearing lipstick. And in case you're wondering if I've been asked for lipstick permission, the answer is yes—to which I issued a resounding *no*. *She* may succumb to peer pressure, but not I. So let's focus right now on peer pressure. For black kids peer pressure may not be any worse than it is for kids of other races, but it certainly has its own distinct flavor.

Let's take what's going on with the rap and R&B music industry. Do you think our kids are walking around with the seats of their pants grazing the ground because you and I wear our clothes that way? Hardly. The explicit language of *some* of these songs is having a profound impact on our kids' development. It's scary to admit, but to some degree, hip-hop is raising our children. It tells our sons how real men act and treat "their" women. It tells our daughters that "they ain't nothin' but bitches and hos." And as it relates to *In the Black,* it tells both genders that they need to be gettin' *paid*—at all costs. That money is where it is and if you ain't got it, you ain't down.

I like using Michael Jordan as an example because he is the endorsement king and our kids, both boys and girls, on some level strive to be like him. So ask your kids the following questions when a Michael Jordan ad comes on the tube.

Do you think he really likes Gatorade?

Do you have any idea how much Gatorade pays him to do their commercials?

What would you think if next week he was doing commercials for Powerade?

The goal here is not to turn your kids against Michael Jordan. I have the utmost respect for Mr. Jordan's business acumen. He has a family and a household to contribute to, and he deserves whatever financial compensation he gets, in my opinion. This is not about him, it is about your son or daughter. Our goal as parents is to turn out kids who spend and save their money wisely. Our goal as parents is to make sure that our kids don't get caught up in being anyone else but the best people they can be. *But please acknowledge that the goal of advertising is to get the product incorporated into your children's identity.*

How to Budgetize Your Teens

As your blossoming young adults begin to understand (through your money lessons) what real money responsibility is, you'll want to upgrade their budgeting skills. A good idea is to have them keep a money diary that outlines how they're spending their money. You've heard "I can't tell you where my paycheck went" before, right? We want to avoid having our teens overdose on this kind of reckless spending.

A money diary can be as simple as having them record their spending in a spiral notebook or as elaborate as using the accounting software on their computer, which is how I keep track of my budget. If you have a computer, you'll have many more teaching opportunities—accounting, checkbook balancing, banking on line, and so forth. If you don't have a computer, don't worry—there's no need to go out and buy one just for this. The point is to track spending to encourage a disciplined approach to money.

At the end of the month, at your family meeting, request that your teens make a financial report outlining how the month has gone, and the status of their financial goals or budget.

Here's a sample budget chart:

MONTH_____

INCOME_____

ALLOWANCE_____

SALARY_____

GIFTS_____

LOANS_____

TOTAL INCOME_____

EXPENSES_____

SAVINGS_____

LOANS_____

   SHORT-TERM_____

   LONG-TERM_____

CHARITY_____

GIFTS_____

AUTO_____

GAS_____

OTHER TRANSPORTATION_____

LUNCH_____

OTHER MEALS_____

VIDEOS_____

MOVIES_____

OTHER ENTERTAINMENT_____

RECREATION_____

TRAVEL COSTS_____

CLOTHES_____

READING MATTER_____

SCHOOL ACTIVITIES_____

MISCELLANEOUS_____

TOTAL EXPENSES_____

Total Income minus Total Expenses =

Cash Flow:_____

Caution: Don't just hand over a sheet of paper and tell your teens to go for it. You want to make sure they are attaching realistic price tags to their line items. This must be a joint effort.

Ethics and Teens

I said earlier that this was a book about values. Well, ethics go right along with values. Ethics may not be a word that your two-year-old can understand, but your teenagers are definitely ready for lessons in ethics and integrity. (And similar lessons can be taught to much younger children. Start by talking about acceptable versus unacceptable behaviors and the lessons inherent in them.) Honesty, integrity, and ethics all go hand in hand. And getting our children off on the right foot in this area will help them avoid many pitfalls later in life. The areas I want to focus on are those that clearly come into play with our kids: property, respect for others, and self-respect.

Sometimes kids take things or abuse things that don't belong to them. Let's say you have two kids, and one collects videos. The other kid decides to borrow one of the videotapes. The owner gets upset, and the borrower says, "Don't ever watch one of my videos without my permission." A fight ensues, and you find yourself in the middle of an ethics argument. This may seem like an ordinary fight between siblings, but there is a valuable lesson to be taught here: *Don't touch things that don't belong to you or the entire family*. This is an ethical matter. If your kids flunk it today, they could be in for bigger problems later on.

In the example above, the borrowing teen may have responded, "But she wasn't even watching it. What's the big deal?" The big deal is that it does not belong to her, period. Never shrug off this kind of behavior. Borrowing, using, taking, or lending something that doesn't belong to you is wrong. It's a violation against another person.

Here are some sample questions you can ask your teens to get the ethics conversation flowing. What would you do if . . .

. . . you found $25 on the locker room floor?

. . . the clerk in the department store gave you too much (or too little) change?

. . . your dad sent you to the store and didn't ask for his change?

. . . your brother was accused of doing something you know *you* did?

. . . you overheard your mother and father discussing a possible divorce?

. . . your best friend told you that she'd stolen something?

. . . your friend told you that his mother was having an affair?

. . . a classmate offered to let you borrow the answer key for a test?

. . . a friend worked at a department store and offered to hook you up?

. . . prior to your mother's going out of town, she told you to be home by 10:00, but you were having a good time at a party, so you strolled in around midnight?

TEACHING THE FAMILY'S FISCAL POLICIES

Debt

Since black debt tends to increase as the income of blacks rises, this section is of particular importance as it relates to our children. One of the ways to safeguard against raising children who are predisposed to debt is by staying debt-free yourself. One needs only to talk to someone who is straddled by debt to understand the incredible impact that "owing" can have on a family unit. You may have a personal experience to call upon. And, if so, then you are well aware of the devastating effects of debt. Do you wish this feeling of helplessness and despair for your children? I doubt it. So, as we say on the basketball court, talk it up—communicate on an ongoing basis about responsible financial behaviors.

Blacks and Credit Cards

Think for a moment about your childhood. Do you remember seeing tons of credit card advertisements on television in the '50s, '60s, or '70s? When you went to visit relatives and stopped at the gas station, did your parents whip out the plastic or pay with cash? Now fast-forward to the world we live in and your own habits. Think about the current state of credit card advertising. If you've watched television lately, you've heard from the big three: Discover Card is constantly upgrading its wonderful "cash back" program. American Express is telling us never to leave home without it. And Visa is reminding us to leave the green card home and instead "bring your Visa" because it's the most accepted plastic worldwide. The ads and hype are everywhere! You can't pick up a magazine on an airplane without a perforated sign-up card falling into your lap. Your new college students can't go to the campus bookstore without encountering a table where their peers are signing them up for their first card.

That's why it's critical to pay attention to your own habits. Your attitudes and habits will have a tremendous effect on your child's attitudes and habits. How often do you use credit cards? What do you use your credit cards for—food, gas, clothes, instant money, books, music, or travel? Why do you or your friends use your credit cards so much? Partly convenience, probably, but more than likely you've fallen victim to the Great Credit Card Seduction: use now, pay later—figuratively and literally.

One of the reasons that we get so deep into credit card debt, I theorize, is the position we think we obtain by owning one to begin with. Remember how happy you were the first time some company sent you an application offering you a credit card? They wrote to you *personally*, told you how much more accepted you would be once you got their card, didn't they? They told you that you could take that 2-by-4 card and conquer the world. And remember when your first card arrived in the mail? *Wow!* I can still feel the smile on my twenty-two-year-old face after I ripped that envelope open and saw my name on that silver card in royal blue. (Yes, they play psychology with the colors, too; why do you think nearly all companies offer *gold* cards?)

In our efforts to be accepted, to be fully integrated into Western society, get our props, have our due respect, some of us have become slaves to the credit card industry. The credit card game is enticing, extremely easy to get into, and very difficult to be emancipated from, if you will—but not impossible. We have to safeguard against grooming another generation of black children who fall into the same traps we or our own parents fell into. Teach your kids the importance of paying for goods and services with cash. Unlike people who advocate that credit cards are just like money, I suggest you teach your children that credit cards are *not* money and that they should not be the preferred payment medium in their lives. Cash is *superior,* and you either have cash money at the time of a purchase or you don't. Credit cards are *not* a substitute because a substitute means equal.

Credit, no matter how you may rationalize it, is more expensive than cash. A $5 pair of shorts costs $5 at checkout (plus tax, of course), but the same $5 shorts paid for with plastic may end up costing between $6 and $10, depending on the institution. So sit your kids down and talk to them about hidden costs, interest, grace periods, and, most important, the price they will eventually pay for adopting the "charge now, worry about paying for it later" attitude.

Charity

We need to teach our kids that sharing with others is truly a blessing, a gift. At least four times a year our family gives things to people who need them, either directly or through organizations such as Goodwill, Blue Santa, or the Salvation Army. Money can be your charitable donation, or you may choose clothes or canned goods. The point is to share what we have with those who may not have as much or anything at all.

When I was a kid, I noticed that sometimes others used to tease poor kids by saying things like "You get your clothes from Goodwill." Let's educate our kids and teach them to be compassionate and not antagonistic toward people who are not as fortunate as they are. I've given some very nice clothes and shoes to Goodwill. They were eventually sold for a fraction of their cost, but they went a long way in keeping people clothed and warm.

A good way to introduce the idea of giving and also build teamwork within your own home is to adopt a charity. At one of your family meetings (discussed later) talk about adopting an organization or a cause that your family will support with time and/or money for one full year. This needs to be a joint decision. Having a discussion about helping people will open your children's eyes to a whole new level of service, and by making it a family endeavor, you will further deepen and strengthen family ties.

If there are five members in your family and each one of you has a different charity in mind, first let each member explain why he or she wants to support that particular cause or organization (making this a nice lesson in persuasive speaking as well). Some family members may concede based on the information presented, but let's say that everyone is holding ground on their choice. What then? Well, what happens in the workplace when there are five different opinions on a particular project? The facilitator must lead a discussion to narrow the choices down. Perhaps the decision will be to make equal but smaller financial contributions to each charity suggested by family members.

Volunteerism

Teaching your kids to give or work without expecting a tangible reward is another one of life's greatest gifts. There are volunteer opportunities all around us— church, school, and community. And don't wait until Thanksgiving or Christmas to get into the spirit of volunteering. Encourage your children to seek volunteer jobs at least three times a year. There's no such thing as being too busy.

In case you need a jump start on ideas, consider the following suggestions: adopt a senior at a convalescent home, visit the cancer floor of your local hospital, organize a neighborhood crime watch program, get in touch with Big Brothers or Big Sisters, Meals on Wheels, or other helpful groups. But remember that you don't need to have a title or be part of an official organization to volunteer your services.

Gift Giving

Another valuable skill to teach your kids is creative and sensible gift giving because sooner or later your kids will want to give someone a gift. This is a perfect opportunity to set a good example. When kids ages one and two are invited to birthday parties, we usually choose the gift ourselves, but when they reach the talking age, it's time to include them in the process. It's important to ask them why they made the choice they did, rather than simply vetoing their selection. The process is the same for ages four through fourteen; it's the nature of the dialogue that's different.

Where gifts are concerned, sensibility is the key

word. Don't buy gifts that are impractical, too expensive, or that have been given zero thought. In other words, why would you encourage your child to buy a four-year-old an answering machine? Or why would you purchase a $200 tennis bracelet for a three-year-old? Or why would you get Granny a pair of running shoes when she has stated that she has no plans to participate in an exercise program? This last example is a good look at impracticality at work. Don't buy folks things because *you* want to inspire them to do something that would make *you* feel better or to do something that they've been saying they're going to do for the last decade.

If I'm not truly motivated to work out, what makes you think that just because a loved one buys me a $300 pair of lightweight, snazzy mountain running shoes that I'm going to find this burst of dedication? I'm not. And neither will others—whoever they are. So don't waste your time, energy, and money encouraging your kids to buy impractical or costly gifts. Gifts should be about thoughtfulness, not the ring of the cash register. Teach your kids to think about the person who is receiving the gift, not whether they'd like it themselves. It's not *for* them.

IS THE MALL STILL OPEN?

I love that episode of *The Cosby Show* where Cliff chides his children about their gift-giving habits— especially to him on Father's Day. He said that they didn't think about what they were going to get him until around 4:00 on Saturday, and then somebody said, "Is the mall still open?"

Teach your kids the importance of planning and

thoughtfulness when it comes to giving gifts. It's not cool to ask Dad for money to get him something for his own birthday, nor is it cool to ask Mom for money for Dad's special day.

For parents who appear to have everything, it's important to hang "wish lists" around the house so that your kids will always have ideas at their fingertips. Children's wishes should go on this list, too, in case someone calls and needs gift suggestions.

Money Matters

CHECKING ACCOUNTS

When is it okay to let your kids open their own account? Well, first of all, your child needs a Social Security number by the time he is one year old. Some hospitals do this at the time of birth, but you should check on this. If your child has been working a summer job and is accustomed to paying for his clothes, recreation, and entertainment, obviously a checking account is something he should already have. In fact, if the kid has a job, it's a great idea.

Most banks have juvenile accounts with very low balance requirements and few if any charges. But don't just tell your child to go and open an account; instead, talk to her about the responsibilities associated with having an account. Go over in detail what having an account means. This is a whole new level of responsibility, complete with charges for insufficient funds, interest, and the possibility of direct deposit. She may decide against it or want to postpone it because she is not willing to make the commitment to balancing the checkbook and keeping up with her spending. If your child says she is not ready for this, please listen. This should not be a forced deal.

TAXES

Teenagers can definitely comprehend taxes. The extent to which you wish to discuss taxes is strictly your choice, but at the minimum you should explain that the government takes a percentage of every dollar he earns. There are books that explain how the Internal Revenue Service (IRS) works and what other deductions are, such as FICA and Medicaid.

I remember my first real job. It was during the summer before I began college. I was told I would be paid $4.50 an hour. That night I grabbed my calculator and figured out how much my first paycheck would be if I worked the full forty hours. My brother had told me that taxes would be taken out and that it wasn't just a straight amount per hour. But when I got my first check and saw that it was next to nothing, I was very upset. Where was the rest of my money? Somebody in accounting made a mistake.

Explain to your kids about the deductions that will be taken out of their checks before they start working. A teenager who is super excited about getting a paycheck will be heartbroken when she finds that her compensation will cover the bus trip home but not much more.

INTEREST

Kids who have learned multiplication can understand at least the basics of interest. Use whatever words you want, but explain to kids between the ages of seven and nine that interest is what a bank pays you to let them hold your money for you. Also show them how different interest rates are paid for different products. For instance, the interest rate on checking accounts may not be equal to that of savings or money market accounts, or certificates of deposit. Explain why the rates differ.

PAYING BILLS

When you sit down to pay your bills, why not invite your kids to participate—especially your teenagers. Otherwise, they might not have an appreciation of what it takes to provide for the family. Let them see that it takes quite a bit of money to put a roof over their heads. Electricity costs money. Cars cost money. Even water costs money. Have a monthly meeting to go over family finances. This is an excellent way to open up communication about the family situation.

If you're really ambitious, give your child the challenge of paying the household bills for one month. This will take your teenagers' level of appreciation and responsibility to new heights because they'll have to employ all the skills they're learning.

FAMILY BANKING

At our house we have a family bank, a central money location that Brittany and I contribute to. Sometimes I'll toss in money that I find vacuuming or money that I have in my workout bag. We use this money to buy pizza or to rent a video that we're both going to watch. The purpose of family banking is to create a sense of unity and oneness. This is something your entire family contributes to, which makes it something you can all talk about and be concerned with.

CREDIT REPORTS

This is a critical issue for black Americans. In general, we tend to have very poor credit ratings or serious credit problems. Our credit demons are not prevalent because we're not good, upstanding citizens; they stem from ignorance or lack of understanding of how the credit system works. And in many cases we don't work hard to repair our credit ratings once they've been damaged. There are many options for repairing bad credit. But you must explore these alternatives. And you must realize that the road back to good credit takes time and patience. So start your kids out on the right foot. You can do so by instituting a credit reporting agency right out of your home. Allow your kids to borrow money from you, but explain that the transaction goes on their personal credit report and that you won't be forgetting or overlooking the fact that they borrowed money. Here are a few guidelines for your system:

With four months (in a row) of consistently good credit reports, they get to increase their line of credit.

If they miss a payment or do something that violates the agreement, they lose a credit rating point.

Here's a sample credit report from the Harris household:

Name: *Brittany*

Date: *April 1, 1997*

Current Rating: **** out of 5

Trans. No./Date	Action	Status
BAd 4/29	Paid $2.50	0 balance
BAd 4/22	Borrowed $2.50 to rent movie	Pay by 4/30
BV 3/31	Paid remaining $2.00 plus $1.00 late fee	Pay by 3/15
BV 3/12	Paid $3.00	Bal. due 3/15
BV 3/1	Borrowed $5.00 for videos	Pay by 3/15

Family Meetings

When I was growing up, we never had family meetings unless somebody died. Then everyone convened at a central location to discuss how things were going to be handled—and the kids were never included in these discussions. I'm not advocating that your six-year-old sit in on a funeral-planning session (not because the topic is death but because of the complicated nature of the discussion), but I definitely think it's important to have meetings where your kids can see group communication at work.

Family meetings provide an opportunity for you and your kids to connect. That's why they are important. Don't call family meetings only for crises. You want to encourage open communication at all times, and if you call family meetings only when something goes wrong, they (meetings) won't be welcomed and may be dreaded. But if your kids know that there will be praise and recognition as well as discussion of some topics important to them, they'll respond more favorably to the meetings.

I suggest a bi-monthly meeting with an agenda of no more than one hour. Place a blank sheet of paper on the refrigerator announcing the next meeting date and asking for kids' written input on agenda topics. You, the parent, are the facilitator of this meeting, which means you'll have to sharpen your organizational and facilitator skills to ensure the meeting runs efficiently. Place a deadline for agenda suggestions—say, four days before the meeting, at 10:00 P.M. Be firm. Don't waffle on the deadline.

Let's say it's January, and your family takes a family vacation the first week in June. One of your agenda topics might be a vacation update. Another topic might be the matter of caring for the car, especially if you have two teenagers who share one car but continually leave it on E (which they think stands for Enough) or in terrible shape with respect to cleanliness or maintenance. You may want to address the possible consequences of not being more responsible. This gives them a chance to hear the grievance and make a public statement to do better if they want to continue to enjoy this privilege. You get the idea. Here are a few more tips for a successful meeting:

- Start the meeting off with praise and recognition.
- Put what you believe to be the most controversial issue in the middle of the agenda.
- Put the lightest issue at the end (vacation plans, announcement of a raise or new baby—careful with this one, etc.).
- Meet in a space where all bodies are spatially equal (around the dinner table or in a circle in the den).
- Require attendance at all meetings.
- Require participation.

- Encourage honest and open dialogue.
- Never allow one person (including yourself) to speak for longer than two minutes at one time.

The following are some operating principles that should be read at the beginning of each meeting:

- No name-calling ("You're such a putz!").
- Keep comments to less than two minutes.
- Ask for clarification if something is said that you don't understand ("I'm sorry, but could you repeat that? I didn't understand" or "What I hear is that you want to be able to use the car every Saturday. Is that what you said?").
- No judgment statements are allowed ("That's so immature." "You have a bad habit of . . ." "You're stupid," and so forth).

Recently I saw an episode of the 1970s sitcom *Good Times*, the one where Florida was given the opportunity to do a commercial and earn $5,000. The family was beside itself with the possibility of bringing that kind of cash into the household. They talked about all the possible ways in which they could use the money but ultimately settled on college education. Now here was a family that was barely getting by, but James and Florida's top priority was their kids' education. How many of us would think about saving *first* if a load of money suddenly fell upon us?

PREPARING FOR THE BIG SEND-OFF: COLLEGE

If you want to celebrate the birth of your new child, set up a trust fund or college fund. In fact, you should start planning for your kids' college educations *before* you give birth. But just in case you didn't set something up before they arrived, you should get to work on it as soon as you catch your breath between feedings. Education is anything but cheap, and it's not getting any cheaper.

According to a recent report done by the Family Economics Research Group of the U.S. Department of Agriculture, to raise a child from birth to seventeen years of age costs $334,000. Obviously, that number does *not* include a college education!

In 1993, the cost to send your kid to a public university for four years was roughly $38,343. Now, applying an inflation rate of 7 percent, that means you'll need about $129,597 for a graduate in the class of 2011. That's $129,597, people! The good news is that unless your child graduates next week, you still have time to do something. And remember, you *can* do something. I'm not here to crucify you for getting a late start, I'm here to tell you to keep your head up and get help today. If you (or whoever is paying for school) have about 40 percent of the total amount on orientation day, you're in decent shape.

Where Will Thou Goest?

Perhaps your children are staunch supporters of continuing their education. Then the question becomes: Where will they go? Private, public, community, junior, black, or white? These are not easy questions for us to tackle, and only you and your family can make this choice. In general, let me say that the quality of education should be your primary goal. I'm amazed at the assortment of reasons given for why kids and parents select one college over another: Family tradition, athletic teams (even when their kids aren't athletes), and social status are among the many.

The question then becomes: "Whose decision is it, anyway?" Believe it or not, I've heard parents say that they will pay for their children to attend only certain institutions, and if they don't want to go to those schools, then they can pay for college themselves. I don't agree with this philosophy. The decision of where your child will be educated during the college years should be a joint one. After all, it is *their* life, you know.

The college years should be the most enjoyable of their lives. It's a time of intense self-discovery and reflection. It's a time to implement all the terrific lessons they've learned as kids. And, finally, it's a time to continue to fine-tune their life plans. It should not be complicated by the necessity of being in the same fraternity as one's father or majoring in the same subject as one's mother. Are you starting to get my point? This is not about you. Please accept this fundamental fact. This is your child's life, not yours. Don't ruin this incredible experience by trying to redo something you goofed up on. Don't taint it by trying to relive that glorious stint in your life. Let go and let your kids have their own college experience.

WORKING THROUGH COLLEGE

Although there is some information that says students who work through college earn lower grades than those who do not, I'm sure students who are extremely involved in campus activities or sports are in that latter group. Don't let statistics dictate your life. If you and your child decided that part-time employment is a viable option, then go for it. As parents you need to understand that working while going to school is difficult. It's stressful and taxing. So if your son or daughter is employed while in school, be prepared to provide a shoulder.

Q. *My son waltzed in and announced that he has decided not to attend college and instead wants to take the money we'd saved for his education and move to Los Angeles to pursue a career in screenwriting. Is he out of his mind?*

A. This is not an easy situation to confront. On the one hand, as parents we want to support our children's dreams and aspirations; on the other hand, we don't want them to risk their money on something that might not pan out. But there are no guarantees in life. The important thing to consider is how serious your son is and how complete his plan is. If you were blindsided by the announcement, then there's a good chance your son hasn't thought it through himself. Go back to my ol' faithful advice: Talk it over openly. There are many successful people who bypassed formal education.

INSTITUTIONS OF HIGHER EDUCATION

Many but not all private colleges are church affiliated, although most do not restrict their admissions to people of that religion. In addition to religion, social status, special needs, and unique talents tend to play a part in our sending or encouraging our kids to attend certain colleges. Some private schools specialize in students who have unique educational needs; they may have emotional disturbance issues, behavioral problems, or learning disabilities. Still others meet the needs of students who possess unique talents, such as in the arts— theater, dance, and film.

If your decision to go private over public is primarily to keep your children away from the so-called lower orders, then I have three words for you: Get over yourself. This attitude will put your children at a distinct disadvantage in the real world. And that, my sisters and brothers, is all I have to say on that matter.

Public schools are clearly a good value for your money, although community colleges generally beat them out financially. Many public institutions have enhanced their academic programs over the last decade, a fact that has many parents considering this option.

Can one make the statement that a private school provides a superior education over other choices? Not at all. It depends on what you mean by a quality education. Remember, we should be seeking quality here. You have to ask yourself: "Why are my kids going to college in the first place?" To give them a competitive edge in the marketplace upon graduation? Because everyone in our family went to that school? Because everyone else's kids are going?

This question must have an honest answer. If the answer is, To enhance their attractiveness to potential employers, you'll be pleased to hear that most employers now realize that where a student is educated is only one of many factors that create an excellent employee. Work experience, recommendations, and campus and community involvement are increasing in importance. And my preliminary research reveals no evidence that individuals schooled at private institutions fare better in the work environment than publicly schooled students. Nor is there any evidence that proves private schoolers lead healthier or more fulfilling and productive lives.

Junior or community colleges are also increasing in popularity. The best junior/community colleges are linked with the state universities. Admission standards and tuition fees are generally lower, which sometimes makes them ideal starting blocks for kids. There are a couple of factors to consider before choosing this route. First, the student population is generally smaller than on main campuses, so classes often have fewer students. Some students find this attractive. The smaller class environment may allow students greater access to professors. Such a setting is often less intimidating than larger campuses. One disadvantage could be that the student who is living at home may experience deep social deprivation.

BLACK OR WHITE?

Upon graduation from high school I had a diverse group of institutions to choose from—black, white, private, and public, and either an academic or an athletic scholarship to all of them. I remember when a teacher encouraged me to attend a particular black university in Texas or another one in Tennessee. I listened intently as she talked about supporting black colleges, and I must say I was in a major dilemma. I could see myself at Spelman or Howard, but I had to consider my athletic career as well. I couldn't simply ignore where I wanted my athletic career to take me; so, I had to weigh more than the quality of the education.

Finally, I realized that there were numerous ways that I could support black colleges without attending one. I could make a financial and a social contribution for the rest of my life. So I chose the University of Texas at Austin. Close enough but not too close to my hometown of Dallas. My family could continue to watch me play, and I could enjoy such things as nice weather, friendly people, and a thriving academic and athletic environment. I was going to be getting a quality education and a chance to develop my athletic talent in one of the top sports programs in the country. This was ideal for me because it met many needs.

Studying Abroad

What an extraordinary opportunity! If your child has the chance to study in another country, he should think carefully before he lets this pass him by. Having traveled to more than twenty countries and having lived in two, I can honestly say that studying abroad is an incredible experience. When I was sixteen, I participated in a student-exchange program. For one month I studied in Cuernavaca, Mexico. I learned a new language and experienced a truly exciting culture. And I would recommend a program like this to anyone. I will encourage my kids to travel and study abroad. Be sure that your child is ready for life outside the United States. Have him do research and find out as much as he can about the culture and language beforehand. There's the library plus great information on the Internet about any country you want to know about.

Reaching a Decision

What I wanted to do above was provoke thought. There are no hard-and-fast answers here, but you would be remiss if you made a decision in haste. Do some research yourself. Have your child narrow her choices to five institutions. Then send her off to gather information—and I don't mean simply school brochures and college guides, I'm talking going to the school, if possible, and checking it out. If that's not financially feasible, call the school and discuss key points. Of course, the ideal situation is always hearing testimonials from a few students or alumni.

What about the decision to stay at home or live in a dorm—in a word, away from home? It may appear that you're saving money by having your college student stay at home, but the savings are not that substantial when you factor in gas, food, and other expenses. Plus, students miss out on a unique experience when they stay home at least one year.

Paying for College

If you're just getting started, now is a good time to speak with a financial planner about your education needs. And if you haven't already thought of it, who says your kids' education is 100 percent your responsibility? Not I. In fact, there are a couple of ways to handle this issue.

First, if you're just dead set on making a contribution, then a reasonable split of, say, 60-40 or 70-30 is advised. I know parents who go broke, get divorced, and become deathly ill—all in the name of paying for their kids' education. There are two ways to avoid these negative setbacks: be wealthy or plan ahead. Take your pick. I'm going to provide a few alternatives for you to consider. But, once again, consult a professional, someone who can supply you with more details and elaboration on all these vehicles. This is just an introduction.

Mutual funds: A portfolio of professionally bought and managed financial assets in which you pool your money along with thousands of other people, hence the name "mutual" fund.

The professional company provides a funds manager who invests the money in different securities such as a combination of stocks, bonds, and foreign funds. Your manager also watches the market for fluctuations in prices.

Advantages: low initial investment (sometimes as low as $25, depending on the company), low risk, and your money is spread out over many areas—so if one security does poorly, another's gain may cover the loss.

Zero coupon bond: a corporate or government security issued at a deep discount from the maturity value that pays no interest during its life. It is redeemable at face value.

Advantages: backed by the corporation or government, low risk, the discount usually makes up for the lost interest during the years that the bond is maturing.

Disadvantages: no interest paid, which means that with inflation the money you receive after redemption may not have been worth the loss of interest.

Corporate bond: A bond issued by a corporation. The bond normally has a stated life and a fixed rate of interest.

Government bond: issued by the U.S. Treasury and considered the safest security in the investment world. There are two categories of government bonds: those that are not marketable and those that are. *Savings Bonds* are not marketable—that is, they cannot be bought and sold once the original purchase is made. These include the familiar Series EE Bonds. You buy them at 50 percent of their face value, and when they mature twelve years later, they can be cashed in for 100 percent of their face value.

Marketable bonds fall into several categories. *Treasury Bills* are short-term U.S. obligations, maturing in three, six, or twelve months. They are sold at a discount of the face value, and the minimum denomination is $10,000. *Treasury Notes* mature in up to ten years. Denominations currently range from $500 to $10,000 and up. *Treasury Bonds* mature in ten to thirty years. The minimum investment is $1,000.

The advantage of any of the government bonds listed is that they are the safest investment with the lowest risk. The disadvantage is that with the exception of the Treasury Bills they tend to have long maturity ranges, and if you decide to cash them in before the maturity year, you'll lose the time and interest already invested in them.

Certificates of deposit: a low-risk investment offered by banks and savings and loan companies. The interest percentage is generally based on the federal interest rate. CDs can be bought for a minimum of three months, and the minimum investment can be as low as $500. The advantage of CDs is that interest rates are generally higher than the bank's regular savings interest rate and can often be linked to a free checking account.

Sources of Aid

There appears to be a general lack of knowledge—not funding sources—when it comes to financing our kids' education. And few high school counselors are equipped to fully inform you or your kids about the many financial aid opportunities available to them. This section gives you a good place to start.

SCHOLARSHIPS

Some scholarships are awarded on merit and others on need—two concepts that can be extremely misleading. Let's start with needy students. If they don't show the kind of scholastic potential that funding sources require, then they may not get the money. And needy is often confused with poor, which may not accurately depict the situation of a needy student—especially one who has a unique familial situation such as unusually high medical bills, more than one student in college, or astronomical expenses. In other words, unless you are the daughter of someone named Jordan or the son of someone nicknamed Q, then you can consider applying for need-based scholarships.

National Merit Scholarships: So much hype surrounds the top 2,000 or so winners that people don't realize that approximately 6,500 students are awarded these scholarships annually. This is one scholarship that counselors tend to keep abreast of; however, your child must take the Preliminary Scholastic Aptitude Test in his junior year in high school to be eligible.

Community, corporate, or sorority/fraternity-based scholarships: There are hundreds of opportunities in this area. Do some research to find out which corporations are awarding scholarships. Most of them are highly publicized or can be found through guidance counselors' files. My suggestion is to have your child write to a specific corporation to get the criteria (and this is also good practice for business writing).

Athletic scholarships: When I tell people that I attended the University of Texas on a full four-year scholarship, the response is always the same: "Wow, you never had to pay for anything? That's fantastic." If you look at an athletic scholarship from a purely financial perspective, yes, it's quite attractive and enticing. But beware of just encouraging your athlete to jump at the first carrot dangled in her face. Nothing in life is free; there's always a price. For athletic scholarships it's *time*. College athletics operates as a business in today's environment. I'm not one of those people who espouse the notion that colleges today are using and exploiting black athletes because, in my opinion, "using" someone means that what they are getting is disproportionately unequal to what they are giving. And I just can't bring myself to devalue free tuition.

In other words, your athlete is offered a trade. When a coach offers your star a scholarship (full or partial), the offer is essentially: You play, we pay. That's what I encourage athletes across the country to realize. I hear so many athletes scoffing about how they're being used to make the university "bank." And I say, "Boy, you're getting to play golf, something you love, and in return they're paying for your food, books, classes, and shelter—for four years!" Nobody's being used. It's a business, period.

So encourage your kids to approach the athletic scholarship situation as a business deal. It's not emotional. Your child is not the only one being offered a scholarship and is just a small piece of the puzzle. There are dangers associated with accepting an athletic scholarship. Yes, the cost of your education may be covered, but athletes need more than money to succeed in college. They need tremendous support. In other words, ask the coach the following questions and listen closely to the answers.

1. What kinds of academic support efforts does your department have for your athletes (tutors, study hall, on-the-road support, and so forth)?
2. How many times a day does your team practice? Hours? Weekends?
3. What efforts are made by your department to monitor your athletes' progress so that they and you know where to avoid a potentially dangerous situation?
4. Are you in contact with professors?
5. How responsive are professors to the rigors of athletic participation?

GRANTS AND LOANS

Before you spend one dime on college education, look into government assistance programs. Some of these are nonrepayable grants; others are low-interest loans made to the student with repayment delayed until after graduation.

Pell Grants: The amounts vary and are based on financial need and college costs. They are available to part-time and full-time students, and they need not be repaid.

Supplemental Educational Opportunity Grants (SEOG): These offer as much as $4,000 a year; they give priority to recipients of Pell Grants and are based on financial need and the availability of SEOG money at the student's particular college. They need not be repaid.

Perkins Loans: Available to both undergraduate and graduate students, they are given for a maximum of $9,000 for four years and must be repaid.

Stafford Loans: These have replaced the Guaranteed Student Loans and are made by commercial lenders. The interest rate is 8 percent for the first four years and 10 percent afterward. The amount borrowed can increase annually as the student progresses through college, with a maximum of $17,250 for undergraduates.

Federal Work Study Program: This federally funded program pays students for work done for the college.

Letting the Eagles Fly

We can joke about being glad "when they finally leave," but the reality is that the actual event is a bittersweet experience. I'll never forget the day I picked up my little brother from my dad's house to take him to college. All I'd heard for the prior three months from both of them was how glad they were to be splitting up, but after we finished packing the car and were about to say our good-byes, both of them were in tears.

No one can prepare you for that day, and no one can make it any easier for you. It's a long process, one that doesn't end when you drop them off and head home. But you must let go, and so must they. One of the biggest mistakes parents make in the college process is making a physical break but not making an emotional one. Your child is no longer in need of your *constant* supervision and watchful eye. In fact, the only way he'll grow and mature is if you cut the apron strings. And I put the onus on you because sometimes they can't. They need your strength now more than ever. So what does letting go look like? Take a look:

Telephone calls: Limit them. Don't be their wake-up calls or their nighttime lullabies. There will come a day when you'll call and she won't be there. Trust me: You'll survive. A good rule is to call maybe once a week, but certainly not every day.

Visits: Keep them short and infrequent. If you're thousands of miles away, this might be easy, but even if you're in the same city, don't be a permanent fixture in your child's dorm room or apartment. If he is truly involving himself in the college experience, he won't have time for you anyway.

Bite your tongue: You've probably been practicing this in your child's last year of high school, but if you haven't, now is a good time to start. When your child gets in a fix, she will ask, "What would you do, Mom?" or "What should I do, Dad?" When she does, don't you dare make this about you. In fact, before you answer any questions, you should ask your child how she is planning to handle the situation and why she has chosen that course. Then and only then (if you just must) do you say how you might have handled it and why. Ideally, you want to provoke thought. To use sentences that will encourage your kids to consider different alternatives. Never, never, never tell your kid what she "should" do.

Let the cookie crumble: How does the saying go? Mess happens? And when it does, the last thing you need to do is clean it up. No matter how difficult it is to watch from the sidelines, you must. This is a tough one and probably my biggest challenge with my college student. But once you do it a few times, it becomes much easier. Your job is just to listen compassionately and offer support. Don't fix it.

Your Child Is Off to College

Wouldn't it be nice if, when we sent the kids off to college, they'd leave home fairly self-sufficient and self-reliant? But actually sometimes, because for some young people, college is their first experience away from home, it becomes quite a costly endeavor for the parents. Well, it's time to tighten the grip a bit and force your kids into a shift of paradigm.

Financial Mistakes Made with Kids in College

LONG-DISTANCE CALLS

Once they go off to college, it doesn't stop. But you don't have to go broke because your kids haven't become the money managers you dreamed they would become. The first rule of long-distance calling is they don't call collect *unless* they are in serious trouble or there's a life-threatening situation. In *all* other situations they should use their own phone cards or telephone service.

If you don't have the heart to institute these measures, at least set simple guidelines such as paying for only two phone calls per month for fifteen minutes each. This means that if your child wants to speak for thirty minutes at one time, the next time you hear from him it will be on his dime.

I find that when parents let kids know they love them but they will not accept astronomical phone bills, kids generally adopt a different mind-set about calling home. They write more or are more aware once they get their parents on the phone. Let your kids know that talking for three hours isn't necessarily a display of love. Another idea is to have them invest in prepaid calling cards.

TRIPS HOME

Well, there's gas or air or bus fare, take your pick. And who's paying? Even if your kids can afford to pay you a visit weekly, don't allow it. Yes, even if you miss them as much as they miss you. We want our kids to develop survival skills and they simply cannot do it running back to their security blanket every weekend. If your child is coming·home every weekend or more frequently, he needs to get a life—and so do you. This isn't exactly preparing him for life without you, or you for life without him.

One of my college roommates had a very close relationship with her mother—so close that her mother would come to our apartment on weekends to do her laundry and would regularly stock our refrigerator with food to last a month. As a result, my friend was not the most responsible person I knew. She didn't have to be: Mama was doing it all.

Additionally, here are things your kids should be mastering while they're away at school.

Budgeting: Students should have enough money to have a checking account (and balance the checkbook) and a savings account. Encourage them to read their statements thoroughly. Banks do make mistakes, and they can be costly.

Applying for credit: We went over this earlier, but students who didn't experience this as a teenager should definitely get a taste of it in college. Even if they get a credit card with a $100 limit (a good credit line), encourage them to take advantage of establishing a credit history. The important thing for them to understand is that they are applying for credit for one purpose and one purpose only: *to establish credit.*

Reading a lease: If your daughter lives in the dorm, why would she need to read a lease? To become knowledgeable for the day that she does rent an apartment or a house. Leases are often lengthy and cumbersome if you don't understand them. So encourage her to stage a mock apartment hunting experience so she can get her feet wet in the process.

Knowing about car insurance: As I mentioned earlier, you cannot keep your kids on your insurance policy once they move out—and the sooner they become adept at establishing policies in their own name, the better.

Registering to vote: I heard on the *Tom Joyner Morning Show* that in 1996 there were 8 million unregistered black voters. That is a shame! Talk to your kids as early as seven or eight years old about voting.

Getting a passport: Traveling abroad is an experience I wish we all could have. Encourage your kids to be intrigued by what takes place on foreign soil. The passport process is fairly simple. It isn't free so prepare your kids for the expense (about $65).

Handling emergencies: What would happen if your son were in a serious accident? Would the officer at the scene be able to locate you immediately? On the back of my driver's license are three names with phone numbers for someone to call if I'm ever in an accident or get amnesia or am lost or whatever.

Checking credit report: If your child has no credit history, request your own report and teach from it.

Filing tax returns: We will assume that since your child had a job by age sixteen, she knows how to complete the appropriate tax forms. But in case she hasn't been employed, it is still important to learn about our tax system in preparation for the day that she will have to file.

Getting traveler's checks: Some kids don't know that traveler's checks are just like money—with a little government protection surrounding them. Encourage your kids to use these whenever they are traveling, such as on spring break, Christmas holidays, and summer vacations.

WHO'S MY ROOMMATE?

There are many practical ways to prepare your new college student for a roommate situation. If you have more than one child, you have the perfect laboratory. Teaching rules of respect and boundaries is paramount. Rarely do two people have the same living philosophies. The new student must develop skills for living with non-family members, which might include things such as conflicting studying patterns, dating habits, money behaviors (lending and borrowing funds and personal property items), and housekeeping preferences. Talk to them about these issues before they step foot on campus.

THEY'RE BA-ACK!

Your parents want you out of the house. They really want you out of the house. They are worried about you, they love you, but God, they want you out of the house.

—BILL COSBY

When Your College Student Returns

Well, you did a good job of getting them out initially, but now it's four (or five . . . or six) years later and they want back in. What do you do? Here are a few considerations before you do anything.

Realize that the person you kissed good-bye on the steps of the dormitory four years ago is probably not the same person standing on your doorstep. It's true. Both parents and kids are guilty of staying frozen in time. Some parents still treat twenty-two-year-olds like the high school graduates who were googly-eyed walking around campus. And twenty-two-year-olds go home sucking their thumbs and holding on to a parent's apron strings. Be prepared for the changes.

Start off with a tall glass of open conversation. This is your best bet. Do not simply accept your child back into your home without an honest discussion about what's expected.

Realize that your child is now your tenant. Before he left he was entitled to bedroom number 2 with the clean sheets and cozy throw pillows. Now your child should be expected to contribute financially to the household.

Should I charge rent? If so, how much? Let's say your mortgage is $1,400 a month. A reasonable expectation is 10 percent, or $140 a month. What a bargain! Where can you get a furnished bedroom and access to facilities for less than $300 in a safe, loving neighborhood? Nowhere that you or I would visit, so your returning child should be thankful for such a deal. *P.S. The IRS does not require that you report their portion as rental income.*

What about food? In some shared households individuals alternate cooking nights, and the cook for the evening is responsible for purchasing the food and beverages for the family. This is one alternative. Another is to build in a food allowance with the rent. If your monthly grocery bill is $500, perhaps 20 percent, or $100, is a good place to start.

What about chores? Of course. At minimum they are required to clean their own rooms. Don't supply maid service.

What about the car? If they use your vehicle, then they pay for their own gas and any damages or maintenance. Also, encourage them to use public transportation or to carpool; it's cheaper than buying a new car. Adding another driver to your auto insurance is also cheaper than buying another car.

Allow a breaking-in period. This is perhaps three to six months to allow your child to get acclimated to her new life, find and get settled in a new job, buy a car, and so forth.

What about rules? Glad you asked. Set them and be clear on them. Remember the 11:30 curfew you had for him when he was a senior in high school? Well, for the past four years he's been staying out until 2:00 or 3:00 in the morning, and sometimes he didn't even come back to his dorm or apartment. What is an acceptable hour to sashay in the door of your home? Do you want him to call if he's not coming in? Can he bring a sweetie home with him for the night? These are all "must discuss" topics.

What about the phone and long distance? It's definitely a good idea for the returning child to get a separate line since his social life has probably been taken to a new level over the past few years. Also, prospective employers may cause the phone to be ringing off the hook. A phone card for any and all long-distance calls is a good idea, too.

How long should they be allowed to stay? This is one of those "Week 1" discussion topics. You may have a child who has no desire to stay at home longer than necessary, and if so, that answers the question. However, if you have one of those children who is bound and determined to hang on until you kick her out, then I'd say six months to a year tops. A year is ample time to find a job and save enough money to move out.

What about insurance issues? Health coverage under a parent's policy ends when the child stops being a full-time student, or sometimes an age is stipulated in the policy. Encourage your kids to get temporary coverage through their universities.

Do I get any tax breaks with this new resident? Although you are providing more than half of your child's support, it is unlikely that you can claim her as a dependent if she is employed. You may get a break if the child earns $2,300 or less during the year. You can also claim someone under age twenty-four as a dependent no matter what the amount earned if the dependent was a full-time student for at least five months of the tax year.

ENTREPRENEURS
OF ALL AGES

Entrepreneur:
The African-American Choice

Nothing gives me a greater thrill than seeing a child get excited about enterprise. With the current climate in the United States, you would think we'd be encouraging our kids to look to themselves for employment security. You can't turn around without hearing about a company's plans for restructure, renewal, revamp, rerenewal, and so forth. The sooner we begin to cultivate and encourage the entrepreneurial spirit in our children, the better off they'll be. Even if they decide to go to work for someone else, they will shoot to the top of their ranks if they possess the E-spirit.

How to Light the Flame

When we talk about encouraging our kids to do something, we're not talking about "making" them do anything. There are subtle ways to light a flame. Let's say your child wants to take a trip with his class and it will cost $100 per child. Instead of giving him the $100, ask him if he can think of creative ways to get his money. You don't say, "Boy, I don't have that kind of money. You'd better figure out something yourself." No, that's anything but inspiring. A better response would be "Hey! That sounds like an exciting trip. What do you say you think of a couple of ways to raise the money to get you there?" Even if your child has never appeared to be very creative or innovative, your charge will challenge him to at least give it a shot. Give him a deadline by saying, "Think about it for a few days and let me know what you come up with after dinner on Thursday. You always have such great ideas." Your child may say "huh" or "I do?" and look at you strangely, but he'll appreciate the compliment and attempt to live out the prophecy.

ENTREPRENEURIAL ACTIVITIES

Below is a list of possible enterprises for your young-sters to take on. The list is by no means exhaustive, but it will at least give you a place to start.

Golf caddie	Santa's helper	Massage therapist
Window washer	Ball shagger	Tutor
Curb address painter	Typist	Birthday clown
Garage cleaner	Greeting card artist	Interpreter
Lawn service person	Messenger/runner	Gift wrapper
Pool service person	Flyer distributor	Editor/copy editor
Carpet groomer	Computer consultant	Laundry sorter
Pet groomer	Freelance writer	Photographer
House sitter	Motivational speaker	Actor
Personal assistant	Personal trainer	Teacher
Mail/paper retriever	Glassmaker	Inventor
Pet/plant sitter	Radio personality	Producer
Bike repairer	Playwright	Snack vendor

A Look at African-American Entrepreneurs

Teaching kids to own their own businesses inspires self-reliance and independence. It also teaches valuable lessons about strategy and problem solving. A word to parents of entrepreneurs: *It's their thang!* Support and encourage, but please don't step in and try to run the show. You defeat the purpose of encouraging them to be entrepreneurial-minded.

In 1996, *USA Today* reported that there were more than half a million black-owned businesses in the United States. That number speaks to the enthusiasm and energy that black folks have for starting and running their own enterprises. One of the areas that we need to improve is in cultivating this spirit early in our kids' development. It is sometimes easier when a child asks for something to just go into your pocket and give it to him, but we ultimately miss out on a great opportunity to teach our kids many lessons, including independence, discipline, and the value of working for your keep.

Positive Reinforcement Charts

Remember the Dr. Feelgood Board earlier in the book? Keep it going. Your little entrepreneurs need to see their names in lights. You may even want to have a family banquet or ceremony to recognize your kids' achievements. This is an excellent way to honor and motivate them to continue to thrive.

Common Mistakes of African-American Kidpreneurs

Getting in over their heads: When you don't know much about business, it's easy to get into the deep end of the pool. We must encourage our kids to bite small pieces of the project and then take on more as they develop more skills for running their business. Remember, responsibility increases with skill level.

Underestimating costs: I'd be willing to bet that every person who has started a business has committed this sin. Our kids will not think about many hidden costs unless we help them think about the smaller details needed to run an effective enterprise, such as markers and poster boards for the lemonade stand.

Overestimating income: Our kids think that because they built it, people will come. While their business may have unlimited potential, teach them that it's always best to overestimate expenses, not income.

Underestimating time: The first thing they must learn is that anything worth having requires effort and that effort equals time. To produce a quality product you must take the time to make sure that it works and will do what you've said it would do.

Spending everything they make: Even as sole proprietors, our kids must understand that the government has given them this great shot at enterprise and therefore it wants its cut. Teach your children to employ the piggy bank system and make sure they pay themselves—but also be sure they pay their bills.

Under/Overpricing: Market knowledge is critical, and it's a valuable lesson to teach young entrepreneurs. Don't let your kid start a business without having some knowledge of what the market is bearing. You will save them tremendous heartache by encouraging them to understand how to price their goods or services.

Lacking confidence: Even though it takes a certain degree of confidence to branch out and start a business, it takes even more confidence once the doors are open.

Confidence is gained by having a solid knowledge of one's products and services as well as their benefits and features. Encourage your child to study her business and know it inside and out.

Buying Black

It amazes me : When we were first granted our freedom, we couldn't get enough of the services of other black folks, but now we're lucky if we even get the chance to do business with our own. When we were sick, black doctors were our mighty good healers. When we were hungry, black folks provided our bread of heaven. When we were troubled, other blacks were our rock in a weary land. But as soon as we bought into our freedom, we stopped looking to us for us.

I've heard people say, "I don't want to hire someone because they're black, I want to hire the *right* person." I couldn't agree more. But don't forget that black enterprises thrived and survived in the early years because black folks supported them.

Now, before you get on me, call my office, or send me hate e-mail telling me how much *you* patronize black folks, I'm not saying that there aren't black folks who support other black folks. I'm saying we need to make a conscious effort to do it more, period. Why? Because I believe ultimately we exist because of the labor of our forebears. We owe it to them and future generations to keep our rich tradition of success going. And we can't do this if we don't support one another.

FIVE PRINCIPLES OF WEALTH BUILDING

1. Get your current money to work for you. Get your kids to invest.
2. Teach them about counting real dollars: Their money must compound at a rate at least equal to the rate of inflation and taxes for them to break even.
3. Encourage them to look to long-term investments such as stocks and property in order to maximize their use of assets.
4. Encourage them to read the money section of the *Wall Street Journal*, *New York Times*, or other publications that are strong in financial information.
5. Pay yourself first.

YOUR KIDS AND THE STOCK MARKET

Encourage your kids, even as teenagers, to invest in one or two strong performers, not twenty. They probably don't have enough money for that much trading. Teach them that building wealth takes time. Encourage them to read the stock reports and then discuss what the points mean. Help them learn that money must multiply at wealth-producing rates of return. Encourage them to choose powerful and stable investments. You don't want your kids to go into a deep depression over a few stock points.

Black Dollars, White Wealth

In January 1962, Pepsi bought four color, full-page ads in *Ebony*. While Pepsi may be drenching with black talent today, thirty years ago ethnic representation was sparse at best. But even then we could see the move toward capturing black consumers. According to a recent survey, black Americans make up 17 percent of the U.S. population. They also represent approximately 20 percent of the soft drink market. That's about $300 million *annually!* So now do you see why we can't turn on a black TV program or one with brown faces in it without seeing a Sprite, Coke, Dr Pepper, or Pepsi commercial? We are giving these companies huge returns on their investments.

WHAT HAPPENS WHEN WE UNITE

During the civil rights era someone issued a challenge: Don't ride the bus to work, to school, or anyplace on Monday, December 5. . . . If you work, take a cab or share a ride, or walk.

The environment of the contemporary decades is dictating the need for blacks to have their own businesses. According to Dr. Claud Anderson's *Black Labor/White Wealth: The Search for Power and Economic Justice,* 95 percent of our disposable income is spent in the white community, and only 2 percent remains in the black community. An April 1994 report further revealed that although $9 billion went to government contracts for black businesses, nearly all were located within the white community; therefore, tax revenue and jobs went to the white community.

Have we forgotten that black businesses during the early post-slavery days survived almost exclusively because of black patronage? Yet we still struggle today with giving black folks our business on a consistent basis. To paraphrase what Anderson says, our failure to practice group economics is keeping black folks in poverty. Our history shows that when we support one another, the results are incredible. According to Manning Marable's *How Capitalism Underdeveloped Black America*, around the mid-1800s the total value of all free black-owned establishments and personal wealth in the United States was at least $50 million—half of which was based in the slave South.

Regarding overcoming the effects of slavery, John William Templeton has the following to say in his book *Success Secrets of Black Executives*:

> Slave mental attitudes extend to the way we perceive African-American owned businesses. We expect them not to offer superior services and products, and we don't regard their owners with much respect. We don't invest in them, and more often than not, we don't even buy from them, even when they're more convenient.

Buy black. It's an investment in our community. It fosters pride and teaches our children an important economic lesson.

One Final Word

Do your best. Raising kids involves tremendous trial and error. Your journey through *In the Black* proves that you want to do the right thing. Just remember: No matter how much they try you, stick with the program and your rewards will be great. And whether they ever admit it, they do appreciate you and they'll thank you one day. Go get 'em!

WAIT!

Got any funny or otherwise interesting stories about your kids and money? Share them with me and other parents! Send your stories to:

> IN THE BLACK $ STORIES
> c/o Fran Harris
> P.O. Box 5806
> Austin, TX 78763
>
> Or e-mail them to: fharris320@aol.com

Subscribe now!

To begin receiving your subscription to the (bi-monthly) *In the Black* newsletter, send a check or money order in the amount of $5.99 to:

> Tall Tree Productions
> P.O. Box 5806
> Austin, TX 78763

If you would like to invite Fran to speak in your city, please make your request by phone at (512) 374-4729.

You can visit Fran at her Web site at:

> http://www.franharris.com